11+

VOCABULARY, COMPREHENSION AND VERBAL SKILLS

WORKBOOK

A **STANDALONE** verbal skills workbook for all 11+, SATs and independent school entrance exams!

11+ VOCABULARY, COMPREHENSION AND VERBAL SKILLS WORKBOOK

based on

THE CADWALADR QUESTS

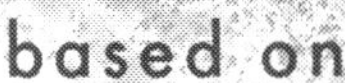

TANGLED TIME

S.L. AGER IN COLLABORATION WITH XLEducation
... because education matters

Copyeditor and proofreader: Leonora Bulbeck
Cover design: Mark Thomas / Coverness.com
Concept, content and interior formatting: S. L. Ager and Sriram Mahabhashyam / xl-education.co.uk

978-1-913753-02-3

www.slager.co.uk

Preface

I first met Sriram Mahabhashyam, founder of XLEducation, when he approached me after reading *Tangled Time*. I then presented to his year five cohort of students. XLEducation's pupils, standards and tuition impressed me. Hence, I am thrilled to collaborate with XLEducation on the first *Cadwaladr Quests 11+ Vocabulary, Comprehension and Verbal Skills Workbook 1*. XLEducation enjoys an outstanding reputation, and in Reading, Berkshire, it is popular because of its proven success with the 11+ tests and excellent provision of long-term 11+ courses, mock exams and online resources.

Vocabulary is crucial to 11+ preparation. This standalone workbook is based on *The Cadwaladr Quests – Tangled Time* and aims to maximise the retention of the novel's rich vocabulary.

We hope you enjoy it!

Sheena and Sriram

How to Use This Workbook

The *11+ Vocabulary, Comprehension and Verbal Skills Workbook 1* is a standalone resource, or for even better results, use it with the novel. The Worksheets closely follow the novel's chapters, offering a wide range of question types, including comprehension, cloze, jumbled paragraphs and sentences, anagrams, synonyms, antonyms and many more. The mixed Revision Tests provide additional practice. The Workbook is suitable for all exam boards.

1 WORKSHEET

SECTION 1 – CLOZE

Choose the correct words from the table to fill in the gaps in the text.

A	B	C	D	E	F	G	H	I	J
unfortunate	friends	repair	childhood	staring	holding	love	fix	done	damage

'Oh no, not you!' Claire stiffened, **1** ____________ at the carpet. 'Wallace! No! No! No!' She thudded down onto bare knees. 'Wallace, what is it? What have I **2** ____________ to you?' she cried as the **3** ____________ scene unfurled. She shuffled along on all fours, creeping closer, afraid of what lay on the floor. Dithering and uncertain, she gingerly lifted him to avoid more **4** ____________ . As she realised it was worse than she'd thought, she almost dropped him. Cradling him, she tried and tried, but it was too late. Her old friend was beyond **5** ____________ . As Claire gazed down at his broken body, her earnest face wore a mixture of **6** ____________ and sorrow. Tears glazed her eyes as fond **7** ____________ memories unfolded before her. Was this repairable? How could she **8** ____________ this accident? She held him in her hand. 'I wonder if I could glue you,' she said, **9** ____________ Gromit in the other hand. 'I'm such a clumsy klutz!' A regretful smile separated the three **10** ____________ .

SECTION 2 – SYNONYMS

Select the word from the options that is closest in meaning to the word in **bold** on the left.

11	**lived**	A. slept	B. resided	C. invaded	D. built
12	**considered**	A. rejected	B. confided	C. lauded	D. contemplated
13	**appealed**	A. attracted	B. bored	C. applied	D. abdicated
14	**cheery**	A. fanciful	B. confident	C. pleasant	D. churlish
15	**gathered**	A. scattered	B. collected	C. graded	D. conveyed

SECTION 3 – SHUFFLED SENTENCES

Rearrange the words to form a meaningful sentence and find the superfluous word.

16 family Christmas together every my very gets

17 not the dirty took pretended I notice how to was place

18 chocolate a small eaten be only in quantities should

19 your mustn't don't he's brother studying irritate while

20 from teeth look you age a over should your after young

2 WORKSHEET

SECTION 1 – COMPREHENSION

Read the passage and answer the questions that follow.

an extract from The Cadwaladr Quests – Tangled Time – Chapter 2. **The Note**

Claire shot upright. Streaks of sunshine sneaked through the gaps in her curtains, **projecting** sparkling **shards** that shimmered onto the wall.

Why's my lamp on? What time is it? she thought, trying to shake the fuzzy **haze** from her head.

It looked too light outside and sounded too quiet inside. **Bleary**-eyed, she cocked her ear towards her door; the silence bothered her. She concentrated harder and listened for the **hectic pandemonium** of morning, only none came. Diving out of bed, Claire snatched her clock. She was shocked to see it had stopped, and for the first time in her young life, she'd overslept.

'Weird, I must have been tired last night; I didn't eat my crisps.'

She'd trodden on them with a loud crunch. In a horrible **tizzy**, hopping and brushing cheesy crumbs from between her toes, she threw on her crinkled uniform, cleaned her teeth and scooted downstairs. She hoped she wasn't extremely late. Surely someone would have called her before they left. She was normally **punctual** and hated being late. **Astonished**, Claire came down to find a **deserted** house, and clean dishes. The kitchen looked just as she'd left it last night.

That's a first, she thought.

Not a **trace** of breakfast or scattered make-up. Amazed by the tidiness, she gulped down some icy milk and wiped her mouth on her jumper. Slamming down the glass, she guessed they'd forgotten to wake her and left for the day. They never failed to surprise her.

'They're a right load of selfish goons,' she complained out loud, gathering her schoolbooks, wishing she'd packed them last night.

Rubbing today's toothpaste, and now milk, off her sleeve, Claire found her Tangle Teezer, and with a couple of strokes, she **tamed** her **unruly** waves. She pulled her hair into a ponytail and grabbed her coat and bag. After going back upstairs, twice, she finally managed to leave the house. Nagged by an unwelcome prickle of **anxiety**, she slammed the door and, **uncharacteristically**, ran all the way to Ben's.

'Odd,' Claire puffed as she knocked again. No one answered. Ben had left for school without her. *That's weird. Why didn't he ring me at home when I didn't show up?* she thought, hurt.

Realising she had no idea of the time, she headed for school, sprinting through the graveyard and up to Gladys's house. Panting, she stopped at the gate. Jack and Thomas sat **abnormally** still, side by side like two **allied sentries** guarding the entrance. Gladys wasn't in the garden, and her front door gaped wide open.

1 Which word in the first paragraph tells us that it is a bright morning?

A. 'sunshine'

B. 'sparkling'

C. 'streaks'

D. 'projecting'

2 Find the antonym of 'peace' between lines 1 and 15.

A. 'fuzzy'

B. 'pandemonium'

C. 'horrible'

D. 'punctual'

3 Which of Claire's actions tells us that she is upset?

A. She drank some milk.

B. She slammed down a glass.

C. She rubbed the toothpaste from her sleeve.

D. She left the house.

4 Which word between lines 20 and 25 tells us that it was unusual for Claire to run to Ben's house?

A. 'unwelcome'

B. 'unruly'

C. 'anxiety'

D. 'uncharacteristically'

5 What did Claire assume was weird with regards to Ben?

A. He had gone to school without her.

B. He was wearing odd clothes.

C. He had forgotten to eat breakfast.

D. He hadn't done his homework.

6 What did Claire assume Gladys should be doing at this time of day?

A. making breakfast

B. ironing clothes

C. hanging out her washing

D. cleaning her bedroom

7 What is another word for 'sentries' (line 28)?

A. guards

B. warriors

C. spies

D. thieves

8 What did Claire have to travel through to reach Gladys's house?

A. a church

B. a school

C. a graveyard

D. a library

9 **What is a 'deserted house' (line 12)?**

A. a house with many desserts

B. an abandoned house

C. a small house

D. a house in the desert

10 **How do we know Claire woke up suddenly?**

A. Claire shot upright.

B. Claire rolled over.

C. Claire hopped.

D. Claire skipped out of bed.

SECTION 2 – WORD DEFINITIONS

Choose the correct definition for the underlined word.

11 **Astonished, Claire came down to find a deserted house, and clean dishes.**

A. crowded; full of people

B. noisy; lively

C. abandoned and empty

D. a desert island

12 **Not a trace of breakfast or scattered make-up.**

A. thrown about carelessly

B. very well planned

C. done with great care

D. forgetful

13 **Nagged by an unwelcome prickle of anxiety, she slammed the door and, uncharacteristically, ran all the way to Ben's.**

A. unnecessary

B. unwanted

C. useless

D. useful

14 **Jack and Thomas sat abnormally still, side by side like two allied sentries guarding the entrance.**

A. quite ordinarily

B. done in a boring way

C. done with unusual quiet

D. quite unusually

15 **Jack and Thomas sat abnormally still, side by side like two allied sentries guarding the entrance.**

A. being acquaintances

B. knowing someone because you work at the same place

C. having the same ideals and goals; working together

D. being mortal enemies

SECTION 3 – COMPOUND WORDS

Underline a word from each set of brackets to make a new compound word.

16	(tea, spun, feet)	(round, pot, tight)
17	(front, into, hall)	(little, way, lounge)
18	(suit, tiny, uneasy)	(door, wide, case)
19	(checked, back, missed)	(yard, customary, about)
20	(phone, person, up)	(go, where, stairs)

SECTION 4 – LINKED WORDS

Select the word from the options that fits best with the words in both sets of brackets.

21 (bee, insect) (doorbell, alert)

A. honey	B. alarm	C. sting	D. buzz	E. noise

22 (lion, tiger) (engine, car)

A. roar	B. miaow	C. purr	D. snore	E. cough

23 (nut, food) (absorb, understand)

A. cashew	B. peanut	C. digest	D. sleep	E. round

24 (electricity, current) (surprise, dismay)

A. voltage	B. shock	C. power	D. anxiety	E. despair

25 (move, relocate) (slot, session)

A. swing	B. alter	C. time	D. shift	E. alleviate

SECTION 5 – ODD WORD OUT

Select the odd word out in each set of words.

26	A. restriction	B. restraint	C. liberation	D. confinement
27	A. gloomy	B. bright	C. dismal	D. dreary
28	A. quick	B. sprightly	C. nippy	D. plodding
29	A. relenting	B. resolute	C. pushy	D. insistent
30	A. stubborn	B. obstinate	C. compliant	D. adamant

SECTION 1 – JUMBLED PARAGRAPHS

Choose the most logical order of sentences to construct a meaningful paragraph.

1
a) I hope to hear from you soon.
b) She is a husky puppy.
c) I am writing to tell you about my new pet.
d) I got her from an animal shelter.

A. a b c d	B. d c b a	C. b a d c	D. c b d a

2
a) I think climatology is interesting.
b) However, many people might find it boring.
c) If you understand it well, you can predict the weather quite accurately.
d) Climatology is the study of weather and its effect on the environment.

A. a b d c	B. d c a b	C. b d c a	D. a b c d

3
a) She called the campsite to reschedule her stay.
b) She was asked to work on Saturday.
c) Her camping trip would have to wait for another time.
d) She was upset because she had already made plans for the weekend.

A. b d c a	B. c d b a	C. d b a c	D. a c d b

4
a) Fantasy books are my favourite.
b) I have loved them ever since.
c) I started reading them when I was ten.
d) They let me escape to different worlds.

A. b c d a	B. c d a b	C. a d c b	D. a b d c

5
a) I arrived at work an hour late.
b) I then had to think of an excuse to tell my boss.
c) I had to catch the 9.15 bus.
d) I overslept this morning.

A. b d c a	B. d c a b	C. c a b d	D. a d b c

SECTION 2 – CLOZE

Choose the word that best completes the sentence.

6 Claire imagined he'd _________ little nonsense.

A. partake	B. instigate	C. tolerate	D. estimate

7 Claire's equine _________ amounted to nothing.

A. enthusiasm	B. experience	C. expectations	D. exultations

8 The trap bumped along the _______ road.

A. deserted	B. desert	C. dessert	D. depressed

9 Twisted trees lined and _________ their way.

A. concerted	B. canopied	C. contained	D. contrived

10 Claire rubbed at her mouth, spitting out specks of _________ dirt.

A. grading	B. grating	C. dirty	D. gritty

SECTION 3 – MISSING LETTERS

Find the three letters that have been removed from the word in CAPITALS. Once these letters are placed back in the word, the sentence will make sense.

11 Jack perched on the man's knee, seeming so CONT Claire felt certain he'd done this before.

A. ton	B. ten	C. hun	D. fin

12 She held tight, stopping herself from SPING out over the trap's side.

A. ink	B. din	C. tri	D. ill

13 The pony's shoes DDED on the road, and sparks flew as the metal struck stone.

A. ski	B. spa	C. the	D. ply

14 *What? Where did that come from?* thought Claire, as an IMPOG bridge towered before them.

A. din	B. hil	C. shi	D. sin

15 Claire's head whirled from side to side, desperate to take in the SPLID vista.

A. ind	B. phi	C. end	D. spe

SECTION 4 – ADJECTIVES

Select the noun from the options that most closely relates to the adjective in **bold**.

16 familial

A. heritage	B. geometry	C. art	D. cosmology

17 ruffled

A. economy	B. feathers	C. absence	D. travel

18 authentic

A. copy	B. artwork	C. paintbrush	D. pen

19 chivalrous

A. barber	B. deputy	C. knight	D. thief

20 linguistic

A. repertoire	B. choreography	C. speech	D. terrain

WORKSHEET 4

SECTION 1 – COMPREHENSION

Read the passage and answer the questions that follow.

an extract from The Cadwaladr Quests – Tangled Time – Chapter 4. **Hidden in Plain Sight**

The museum exuded a quaint and **parochial atmosphere**, and although it was large and **housed** some **unrivalled antiquities**, its tired **veneer** needed **investment** and modern **refurbishment**.

The Gwalch Gem bracelet lay in a low-key glass case, its resting place for many years. This innocent home was a perfect disguise for its **dazzling supremacy**, the power it granted its wearer recognised by only a rare few.

To the average **spectator**, the bracelet passed as a pretty piece of gold-and-emerald jewellery. Nice but nothing special or, indeed, **priceless**, its real value and power **deliberately** concealed. The Keepers engineered it this way, intending **minimal** attention to be drawn to their secret force. They **shunned** bulletproof glass and laser-beam protection, and purposely **stowed** the gem in an open, public place. There they could guard it, and no one could wear it.

Mostly it was local schools and **pensioners** who visited this museum. A lack of modern **installations** did not attract **the masses** but rather just a **meagre** trickle of local people and **hordes** of bored schoolkids. This humble museum, tucked away in an **inconspicuous** part of town, proved the perfect resting place for the Gwalch Gem bracelet.

'Come on, you lot, look lively! Switch off your phones, and if anyone's chewing gum, please **refrain** by getting rid of it in that bin over there,' ordered Mr Hollie.

Mr Hollie taught 10J history, and Josh Drane didn't **faze** him. No, indeed. **Hence** the school **consenting** to Drane's presence today. Mr Hollie had **assured** the headmistress he could handle him, so she had relaxed the rules, hoping the **gesture** of **independence** might improve Drane's **attitude** and, moreover, his behaviour. Mr Hollie had decided that if it came to it, he would **flex** his **authoritative** muscles today. This group was **infamous** for its **notoriously** challenging behaviour. The headmistress was often called in to **monitor** tricky lessons. Today she had entrusted him to take this **problematic** class on the field trip, and he was **determined** to impress her.

Drane, Rebecca and their **dubious cohort reluctantly trudged** after their teacher. They spat out gum and threw drink cans into an overflowing bin at the museum's **unremarkable** entrance.

1 How could the museum be improved?

A. through demolition

B. through restocking

C. through refurbishment

D. through downsizing

2 What does 'low-key' mean (line 3)?

A. modest

B. exuberant

C. grand

D. cheap

3 Why was the glass case the perfect disguise for the Gwalch Gem bracelet?

A. The gem was very shiny.

B. The gem was very expensive.

C. The gem was worth more than the glass case.

D. The gem was an object of great power.

4 Why was the gem concealed in such an unassuming manner?

A. to provide the Keepers a chance to test their skills

B. to not draw attention to the gem

C. to use magic instead of technology

D. to wait for the right person to wear it

5 Which word between lines 1 and 15 is the opposite of 'noticeable'?

A. 'quaint'

B. 'parochial'

C. 'shunned'

D. 'inconspicuous'

6 What did Mr Hollie tell the students to do?

A. stop talking loudly

B. switch off their phones

C. wake up

D. throw away their rubbish

7 Why did the headmistress allow Drane to go on the trip with the school?

A. Mr Hollie paid her.

B. Drane had excelled in schoolwork.

C. Drane asked her politely.

D. Mr Hollie promised he could handle Drane.

8 What is the meaning of 'infamous' (line 21)?

A. incredibly famous

B. infallible

C. well known for doing bad things

D. shunning fame

9 What did the headmistress often have to do in regard to this group?

A. She often had to help monitor the group.

B. She often had to expel the group.

C. She often had to give the group homework.

D. She often had to grade the group's homework.

10 Which word in the second part of the text tells us the students didn't really want to follow Mr Hollie?

A. 'refrain'

B. 'notoriously'

C. 'problematic'

D. 'reluctantly'

SECTION 2 – WORD DEFINITIONS

Select the most appropriate definition from the options provided for each word in **bold**.

Class 10J were chattering loud, raucous nonsense and fidgeting incessantly. Boisterous and impossible to control, they chucked rubbish and messed around as the ancient school bus limped along with the rush hour through town. Disobeying numerous cautions to put away their phones, they sniggered at photos and texts, hiding them from view.

11 raucous

A. conscientious and caring

B. wild and disorderly

C. relating to the roars of wild animals

D. neat and well organised

12 incessantly

A. quickly

B. thoroughly

C. incoherently

D. continuously

13 ancient

A. of or relating to ants

B. old

C. relating to elderly people

D. unusually important

14 numerous

A. many in number

B. far in distance

C. heavy in weight

D. large in volume

15 cautions

A. hesitations

B. considerations

C. warnings

D. priorities

SECTION 3 – ANAGRAMS

Rearrange the letters of the word on the left to make a suitable word for the sentence on the right.

16	PREFECT	He found the ☐☐☐☐☐☐☐ place to hide his treasure.
17	MUG	Please, don't chew ☐☐☐ in class.
18	NIB	Remember to throw the wrapper in the ☐☐☐.
19	CLOUD	I was told he ☐☐☐☐☐ get the job done.
20	LURES	I always try to follow the ☐☐☐☐☐ of the road while driving.

SECTION 4 – LINKED WORDS

Select the word from the options that fits best with the words in both sets of brackets.

21 (thunder, lightning) (escape, dash)

A. rain	B. run	C. bolt	D. drift	E. sprint

22 (person, associate) (workplace, corporate)

A. classmate	B. colleague	C. greet	D. board	E. office

23 (coil, helix) (descend, decline)

A. spiral	B. twist	C. plummet	D. ascend	E. plunge

24 (categorise, arrange) (binder, portfolio)

A. order	B. index	C. file	D. box	E. case

25 (instructions, information) (temporary, momentary)

A. fugitive	B. passing	C. mandate	D. brief	E. contention

SECTION 5 – SPELLING ERRORS

Select the word in each group that has not been spelled correctly.

26	A. arrogant	B. superior	C. concieted	D. disdainful	E. humble
27	A. profitiency	B. efficiency	C. competence	D. productivity	E. capability
28	A. kindly	B. decently	C. graciously	D. generously	E. courtoesly
29	A. excellent	B. remarkable	C. exeptional	D. outstanding	E. marvellous
30	A. racuous	B. meagre	C. decrepit	D. pertinent	E. attuned

SECTION 1 – HOMOPHONES

Select the most appropriate option to complete the sentence.

1 I _____ the ball _____ the hoop.

A. thorough, threw	B. threw, through	C. threw, thorough	D. through, threw

2 The trawler _____ to catch a big _____ today.

A. ought, hall	B. hall, aught	C. aught, haul	D. ought, haul

3 The _____ of the tree _____ me on the head.

A. bows, court	B. bows, caught	C. boughs, caught	D. boughs, court

4 The waiter _____ two plates of food.

A. bore	B. boar	C. broad	D. bare

5 He had a certain _____ for crafts.

A. flour	B. flyer	C. flare	D. flair

SECTION 2 – PARTIAL ANTONYMS

Complete the antonym of the word on the left.

6	distracted	_ T T _ _ T I _ E
7	liberate	C _ N F _ N _
8	enmity	F R _ E N _ S H _ P
9	immediate	_ R A _ U A _
10	credible	U _ B E L _ E V _ B L E

SECTION 3 – SPELLING ERRORS

Select the word in each group that has not been spelled correctly.

11	A. sarcasm	B. stedfastly	C. stifled	D. sophisticated	E. surreal
12	A. uncany	B. unusual	C. usurped	D. unfulfilled	E. unfathomed
13	A. roughly	B. reassuringly	C. reactivly	D. reactionary	E. retain
14	A. becoming	B. beguiling	C. beckonning	D. beginning	E. belittling
15	A. grubb	B. grinning	C. greatly	D. greenery	E. grating

SECTION 4 – ODD WORD OUT

Select the odd word out in each set of words.

16	A. undetectable	B. invisible	C. unnoticeable	D. conspicuous	E. hidden
17	A. reveal	B. conceal	C. shield	D. screen	E. shelter
18	A. impassable	B. untraversable	C. obstructed	D. impenetrable	E. navigable
19	A. accumulation	B. pile	C. smidgen	D. mass	E. abundance
20	A. replied	B. pretermitted	C. retorted	D. responded	E. answered

WORKSHEET 6

SECTION 1 – COMPREHENSION

Read the passage and answer the questions that follow.

an extract from The Cadwaladr Quests – Tangled Time – Chapter 6. **Above and Below the City**

Incapacitated with revulsion, she pictured a bed of stinging insects in the dirt beneath her. Forcing herself forward, sweating with terror, she crawled on, **straggling** behind Gwilym and Jack, trying not to touch anything alive with her hands and yelping each time she thought she did.

'Keep going. Keep going,' she chanted, **coaxing** herself **grudgingly** forward. 'How long is this tunnel? Please. I hate this. How long is it?' she asked Owain, panic rising further as dirt and dust fell down into her eyes and mouth.

'We are nearly there; it is short,' replied Owain.

'Calm, Claire, calm,' she told herself, **gagging** on a mouthful of dirt.

Up ahead, Gwilym was waiting for her. She increased her crawling speed, **placated** at seeing him and at a glimpse of Jack's **deliriously** happy tail. In front of Gwilym, she could see a handleless wooden **hatch** blocking their way.

'Jack, back!' Gwilym ordered.

The knight, restricted by the tunnel's size, squared his **bulk** against the wood and **shouldered** the **barricade**, pushing it inwards, enabling his fingers to curl around its edge. Grappling for a better **purchase**, he finally managed to **lever** it out of the way. Claire almost **butted** Gwilym out through the opening as she pushed forward, gasping for air. She shot out, landing face down on yet another dirty floor.

The tunnel had opened into a dark, **austere** room, now partially lit by Owain's torch. He found an old-fashioned light switch on the wall, and a **muted** yellow light glowed softly, partly **illuminating** their features.

Shelves stuffed with antiquities – **conserved articles** of all shapes and sizes – surrounded them, covered in a thick layer of dust, seemingly untouched for years. Claire knelt, spitting out and blinking away dirt. A covering of filth **speckled** Jack's coat. Sneezing and snuffling, he shook the grime off in the way only dogs can, twisting and shaking in opposite directions from nose to tail, **coating** Claire in the **process**. She laughed as she brushed it from her sleeves, and was overcome by an urge to hug him, so she held him close, kissing his dirty nose.

Standing up slowly, she absorbed her new surroundings. Yesterday she wouldn't have **entertained** that smothering hole of a tunnel; she would have refused point-blank. *I can do this*, she thought, staring steadfastly at the two men and Jack, **bracing** herself for whatever came next.

1 Find the word in lines 1 to 5 that tells us Claire was unable to move.

A. 'incapacitated'

B. 'straggling'

C. 'coaxing'

D. 'grudgingly'

2 How was Claire able to keep on going forward?

A. She pinched herself.

B. She moved as fast as possible.

C. She coaxed herself.

D. She derided herself.

3 Which word between lines 5 and 20 tells us that Claire was calmed by the appearance of Gwilym?

A. 'placated'

B. 'deliriously'

C. 'shouldered'

D. 'gasping'

4 How did Gwilym get past the barricade?

A. He burned it down.

B. He levered it out of the way.

C. He rammed it.

D. He kicked it down.

5 Which word is used to describe the room as being very plain in appearance?

A. dark

B. dirty

C. austere

D. orderly

6 Which word between lines 15 and 20 tells us about the quality of light emitted?

A. 'partially'

B. 'old-fashioned'

C. 'muted'

D. 'conserved'

7 How can we tell that the objects in the room had not been used in a long time?

A. They were old-fashioned.

B. They were broken.

C. They were covered in cloth.

D. They were covered in dust.

8 How did Jack get rid of the dirt covering him?

A. He rolled on the ground.

B. He splashed in water.

C. He twisted and shook in opposite directions.

D. He ran in circles.

9 How has Claire's attitude changed?

A. She has a stronger willpower to get things done.

B. She is more afraid than ever before.

C. She is more short-tempered than before.

D. She has a more careless attitude.

10 In line 27, it says that Claire was 'bracing herself'. What exactly was she doing?

A. She was putting on armour.

B. She was trying to calm down.

C. She was preparing for injuries by making leg and arm braces.

D. She was mentally preparing herself for any difficulties.

SECTION 2 – COMPOUND WORDS

Select the option that forms a compound word once the blank is filled in.

11 Their flight took longer than expected due to a stop ______ in Dubai.

A. up	B. over	C. go	D. out

12 He needs to get up to date with his ______ work before the end of term.

A. house	B. term	C. school	D. problem

13 They decided to go on a ______ trip to travel across the country.

A. road	B. day	C. car	D. holiday

14 I had to sit on the ______ seat because my parents were in the front.

A. front	B. side	C. over	D. back

15 Take a look at this new ______ site I found.

A. building	B. web	C. net	D. construction

SECTION 3 – WORD DEFINITIONS

Write the correct word next to the definition from the options provided.

A	B	C	D	E
dumbfounded	babble	vacant	palatial	prominent

16	to talk very wildly and quickly	______________
17	famous and held in great esteem	______________
18	overly grand and impressive in appearance	______________
19	greatly astonished by something	______________
20	unoccupied or deserted	______________

SECTION 4 – ADJECTIVES

Select the noun from the options that most closely relates to the adjective in **bold**.

21 **factual**

A. teleplay	B. blockbuster	C. documentary	D. sitcom

22 **situational**

A. director	B. comedy	C. script	D. show

23 **tenacious**

A. detriment	B. disorder	C. deterrent	D. determination

24 **ethical**

A. conscience	B. condolence	C. conservatory	D. conference

25 **willing**

A. volatility	B. voltage	C. volume	D. volunteer

SECTION 5 – RHYMING

Find a word that rhymes with the word on the left to complete the sentence.

26	haggling	Stop S T R _ _ G _ _ N G behind us and catch up.
27	hoaxed	He C _ _ X _ D the dog out with a piece of meat.
28	smudge	Try not to hold on to a G R _ _ G _ for too long.
29	hilarious	The dog was D E L _ _ _ _ U S with excitement when he saw me.
30	rasped	She G _ S P _ D for air after surfacing from the water.

SECTION 1 – ANAGRAMS

Rearrange the letters of the word on the left to make a suitable word for the sentence on the right.

1	STANCE	They made their ☐☐☐☐☐☐ of the hill in the morning.
2	REACTS	There were no ☐☐☐☐☐☐ of the intruder anywhere.
3	REMAIN	I wanted to earn a degree in ☐☐☐☐☐☐ biology.
4	PLATES	Maize is considered a ☐☐☐☐☐☐ food in many countries.
5	MELONS	I like ☐☐☐☐☐☐, although they're quite sour.

SECTION 2 – CHANGE ONE LETTER

Change just one letter in the word on the left to create a new word that matches the description given.

6	blurred	spoke in a disorderly, incoherent way	________________
7	butter	to talk in an angry yet quiet manner	________________
8	baiting	being patient for something to happen	________________
9	decline	to lean back in a comfortable chair	________________
10	request	a property or legacy given to someone through a will	________________

SECTION 3 – CLOZE

Use the underlined words from the text to complete the sentences.

Drane never underestimated any Instinctive, knowing too well that appearances could deceive, but his confidence in their prodigious plan prevailed. His master would soon return to reclaim the bracelet that held the Gwalch Gem; the bracelet would soon be theirs again.

11	He had a _________ imagination, able to create fantastic works of art in a short time.
12	They _________ her tenacity, expecting her to give up in the first week.
13	She is known to _________, so don't believe everything she says.
14	I will _________ my rightful place as heir to my father's company.
15	Her plan to take over from her boss _________ in the end.

SECTION 4 – ANTONYMS

Choose the word on the right that best matches the antonym to the word on the left.

16	judiciously	A. fervently	B. foolishly	C. improperly	D. incredulously
17	safeguard	A. store	B. monitor	C. jail	D. jeopardise
18	specifically	A. preparedly	B. safely	C. jovially	D. vaguely
19	ownership	A. privatisation	B. commerciality	C. consumerism	D. relinquishment
20	undesirable	A. unenviable	B. dreadful	C. exceptionable	D. preferable

SECTION 1 – COMPREHENSION

Read the passage and answer the questions that follow.

an extract from The Cadwaladr Quests – Tangled Time – Chapter 8. **A Knight's Tale**

Upstairs in the museum's office, Rebecca lay dribbling onto the cushion of a tatty chair. Josh Drane perched on its arm, seeming to nurse her so **convincingly** that Mr Hollie had left them with the curator's wife and rushed back to check on his class in the cinema. In the **cramped** office, a **composed** and **collected** Marjorie Evans carefully observed Drane. She was always a patient woman, and her demeanour remained **unflappable** and reticent. Playing cat and mouse, they waited, poised and silent. **Opposing** Instinctives knew the threat of each other's presence.

The drugged girl's **palpable trepidation** filled the **inadequate** space. Rebecca lay **incapable** now, the **dose** of chemicals **asserting** their **comprehensive** control. She would listen only to Drane and, once recovered, would remember nothing.

Outside the office, in the exhibition hall, the boy who had sneaked from the back of the cinema line earlier **loitered** amongst the glass cases. Surreptitiously checking the time, he feigned interest in the exhibits, **imitating** an ordinary, interested student and not the **planted decoy** and Mal-Instinctive that he was.

He watched the second hand sweep twice around the museum's giant clock face. Then, using his full body weight, he shoved a glass exhibit case as **forcibly** as he could, continuing to rock it back and forth.

Upstairs in the security centre, the **flabby** guard, Dave, visibly choked as the alarm rang out.

'Come in, Bert, come in,' he spluttered into his walkie-talkie, spraying a shower of crisps from his mouth. Wiping his mouth on his sleeve, he **heaved** himself up to his feet.

'What is it, mate?' Bert's voice crackled over the radio.

'Number one five eight, the alarm's going off. I can see a lad rocking the case,' replied the guard, spattering crisps again. 'I'll meet you there.'

He brushed crumbs off his **portly** stomach, puffed out his chest and donned his guard's cap. Case 158 was an awfully long walk from the security room. Normally, he'd **gripe** at the prospect of unwelcome exercise, but right now, he didn't mind at all. So excited at his chance to play the hero, he broke from his **dallying** into a wobbly trot. As he **waddled** off to help Bert with the boy, his fleshy **paunch** of a belly sloshed from side to side, like an overfilled beach ball.

1 **What is Dave's belly compared to?**

A. a church bell

B. a beach ball

C. a bowling ball

D. an iron pot

2 **What is meant when it says Josh was 'seeming to nurse' Rebecca (line 2)?**

A. Josh was pretending to be a nurse.

B. Josh was wearing a nurse's uniform as a disguise.

C. Josh was pretending to take care of Rebecca.

D. Josh was training to be a nurse.

3 What about Marjorie's character allowed her to understand the situation more clearly?

A. Marjorie is level-headed.

B. Marjorie is very suspicious.

C. Marjorie is sceptical.

D. Marjorie is deceptive.

4 What is meant by 'playing cat and mouse' (line 5)?

A. keeping someone interested in the conversation

B. continually interrupting someone's speech

C. trying to defeat someone by confusing or tricking them

D. deliberately confusing someone and getting them to agree to something

5 Which word in the second paragraph tells us that the drugs have affected Rebecca completely?

A. 'asserting'

B. 'palpable'

C. 'comprehensive'

D. 'recovered'

6 What type of crime did the boy who sneaked out of the cinema plan to commit?

A. murder

B. theft

C. vandalism

D. kidnapping

7 What law of physics did the boy use to move the glass case?

A. velocity

B. mass

C. momentum

D. traction

8 Which word tells us that the security guard is out of shape?

A. 'loitered'

B. 'imitating'

C. 'flabby'

D. 'dallying'

9 What did Dave do to appear more authoritative?

A. He puffed out his chest.

B. He marched towards the incident.

C. He started shouting orders.

D. He put on his name tag.

10 **Why didn't Dave mind getting exercise in this situation?**

A. He wanted to use his baton.

B. He wanted to show his badge.

C. He wanted to be a hero.

D. He wanted to lose some weight.

SECTION 2 – WORD DEFINITIONS

Select the most appropriate definition from the options provided for each word in **bold**.

<u>Opposing</u> Instinctives knew the threat of each other's <u>presence</u>. The drugged girl's <u>palpable</u> <u>trepidation</u> filled the <u>inadequate</u> space.

11 opposing

A. in conflict

B. allied

C. neutral

D. indecisive

12 presence

A. a great distance from someone

B. to send gifts

C. physical proximity

D. to be vague about your whereabouts

13 palpable

A. intangible

B. insubstantial

C. to process wood pulp into paper

D. substantial and noticeable

14 trepidation

A. anxiety or apprehension

B. relaxation or tranquillity

C. having no doubts

D. to have phobias

15 inadequate

A. sufficient

B. to actively sabotage something

C. to have difficulty in time management

D. less than what is needed

SECTION 3 – SHUFFLED SENTENCES

Rearrange the words to form a meaningful sentence and find the superfluous word.

16 the loitered building suspects around the and

17 an player feigning when injury football the criticism for received

18 he would brother imitated often his

19 not I'm plants gardening learning the names though like when even I all interested in different of

20 I birds playing although in puddles water watched of the

SECTION 4 – SYNONYM GROUPS

Select the group of words that are the most similar in meaning.

21
A. lone, solo, unaccompanied, solitary
B. reveal, show, conceal, highlight
C. unexpected, presumed, unpredicted, surprising
D. familiar, similar, friendly, unknown

22
A. bottom, under, pinnacle, subterranean
B. command, reprimand, chastise, attend
C. scale, ascend, clamber, climb
D. struggle, excel, persevere, rescind

23
A. slippery, slithery, rough, smooth
B. quickly, presently, promptly, leisurely
C. haste, rush, hurry, relax
D. descend, decline, drop, subside

24
A. shut, close, open, barricade
B. stranded, isolated, alone, surrounded
C. repeatedly, often, regularly, continually
D. yield, break, resist, fail

25
A. tenacious, persistent, determined, dogged
B. refuse, invalidate, accept, decline
C. submit, buckle, collapse, defy
D. impatient, indifferent, restless, avid

SECTION 5 – HOMOPHONES

Choose the word that corresponds to the correct spelling for the given definition.

26	occurring one after another	serial	cereal
27	inheritor	air	heir
28	military title	kernel	colonel
29	to interfere	meddle	medal
30	to enhance	compliment	complement

9 WORKSHEET

SECTION 1 – MISSING LETTERS

Find the three letters that have been removed from the word in CAPITALS. Once these letters are placed back in the word, the sentence will make sense.

1 The painting was **AS**, so I righted it.

A. lan	B. kew	C. anc	D. ede

2 The old factory appeared to be **ABANED**.

A. nde	B. ndo	C. don	D. ban

3 She **TREED** in the cold breeze.

A. emb	B. lmb	C. del	D. mbl

4 He spent the long summer afternoon **TING** away in the garden.

A. ail	B. oil	C. eil	D. lin

5 Much **MERRIT** was had at the Christmas lunch.

A. rim	B. min	C. men	D. ent

SECTION 2 – CLOZE

Choose the most suitable word to fill in the gaps from the corresponding set of brackets.

Gwilym realised the Master's aggressive force had been **6** ____________ *(distilled, diluted, deliberated, deserted)* significantly between the two knights; his strength, sliced in half, was **7** ____________ *(infamous, incoherent, inferior, infallible)*. One-on-one, the traitorous brother, Dewi, was hugely **8** ____________ *(competent, contentious, compromised, concise)*, yet he could not **9** ____________ *(surmise, smite, perish, peruse)* both knights together. **10** ____________ *(Comforted, Confused, Combined, Conflagrated)*, Gwilym was certain Owain and he could prevail.

SECTION 3 – VOCABULARY IN CONTEXT

Select the most appropriate option that matches the meaning of the word underlined in the sentence.

11 'Owain, he is using our minds to inflict terror on our bodies.'

A. Terror is being caused by their minds.

B. Terror is being negated by their minds.

C. Terror is being welcomed by their minds.

D. Terror is being monitored by their minds.

12 'He has insufficient strength for two.'

A. He has the wrong kind of strength.

B. He has enough strength.

C. He does not have enough strength.

D. He has the strength of two people.

13 As they lay in the basement's dank filth, their monstrous ordeal gradually subsided.

A. They had to fight a monster.

B. Their ordeal was difficult.

C. Their ordeal was fun.

D. Their ordeal was rare.

14 'Nothing will stand between Dewi and the bracelet.'

A. Dewi would not let anything stop him from getting the bracelet.

B. Dewi would not let anything stand next to her while she was wearing the bracelet.

C. Nobody was standing in between Dewi and the bracelet.

D. Something was stopping Dewi from obtaining the bracelet.

15 A babble of unintelligible words emanated from the room.

A. The words were of a low intelligence.

B. The words were coded.

C. The words were spoken quickly.

D. The words were impossible to understand.

SECTION 4 – PARTIAL ANTONYMS

Complete the word on the right so that it means the opposite of the word on the left.

16	CACOPHONY	H _ R _ _ N Y
17	RUCKUS	P _ _ C _
18	UNFATHOMABLE	U N _ _ _ S _ A _ _ A B L _
19	INARTICULATE	E L _ _ U _ N T
20	ALTERCATION	A _ R _ E M _ _ T

SECTION 1 – COMPREHENSION

Read the passage and answer the questions that follow.

an extract from The Cadwaladr Quests – Tangled Time – Chapter 10. **The First Cut**

The Master had studied Claire as she had grappled with her fear and had finally entered the museum's office, where her sister was held **captive**. Instinctive or not, he had **concluded** this plain young female posed no real threat.

He had surveyed the grand old hall, casting his **vulture's leer** into every **conceivable** space. His highly trained boys **consistently** performed with fail-safe precision; he accepted nothing less. Drane had chosen a suitable hostage, and the old knights Gwilym and Owain, albeit unwilling, had succumbed as planned.

Dewi, the Master, looked sharp. His **tailored** suit and handmade leather shoes **complemented** his lean frame and wide shoulders. Athletic, sculpted muscles rippled discreetly beneath his crisp, **starched** shirt. A hint of **exclusive cologne** followed him. Thick hair, **styled** in **cutting-edge** London **salons**, striking eyes and snow-white teeth **beguiled** everyone he met. His suave disguise was most **persuasive**. When he smiled, everyone yearned to know him, but right now, he didn't aim to fool anyone. The true Dewi emerged.

The Gwalch Gem bracelet was within his grasp. His **covetous** glare finally locked on to it; his fingers itched to wield its power once again. The power he would use to manipulate time to **influence** and **exploit** the world for his gain.

Eerie and **ghoulish**, he appeared to almost skate across the deserted hall towards the bracelet. A conceited pout replaced the thin, **fiendish** line of his lips. Tilting his head, he paused, savouring the moment as he reached into his pocket for the tiny metal box. His long, slender fingers opened the smooth lid and removed the Cutter. He twirled the tiny arrow in his manicured fingers. *How can something so **flimsy** and dull deliver such a great prize? Yet it will*, he thought.

His greed and spirits soared as he leaned over the glass case, marvelling at the gem it contained, its deep green coupled with the Welsh gold Gwilym had mined. He **salivated** as if **embarking** on a **gourmet** feast, his entire being **devouring** the scene before him.

Holding the arrow, his right hand moved towards the glass as his left hand **simultaneously** crawled along the case's edge.

1 **Which word in the first paragraph tells us that Claire was struggling with her feelings?**

A. 'studied'

B. 'grappled'

C. 'finally'

D. 'concluded'

2 **Find the antonym for 'free' within the first two paragraphs.**

A. 'captive'

B. 'instinctive'

C. 'conceivable'

D. 'trained'

3 What did the Master surmise about Claire?

A. He surmised that Claire was a formidable foe.

B. He surmised that Claire was agile but not strong.

C. He surmised that Claire was smart but not fast.

D. He surmised that Claire was not a threat.

4 What does the comparison to a vulture say about the Master's personality?

A. He is exploitative.

B. He is kind.

C. He is unstable.

D. He is benevolent.

5 What is the most accurate way of describing Dewi's dress code?

A. dishevelled

B. anachronistic

C. elegant

D. casual

6 What type of salons did Dewi prefer?

A. fashionable and innovative salons

B. old-fashioned salons

C. barber shops

D. beauticians

7 Which word between lines 5 and 15 tells us that Dewi's appearance was the exact antithesis of 'repulsive'?

A. 'cutting-edge'

B. 'beguiled'

C. 'covetous'

D. 'ghoulish'

8 Why did Dewi want the Gwalch Gem bracelet?

A. He thought it would be a nice accessory for his outfit.

B. He wanted to destroy it.

C. He wanted to give it to someone as a gift.

D. He wanted to use it to gain vast power.

9 Select a suitable word for the type of movement Dewi made to get to the gem.

A. hover

B. glide

C. crawl

D. scamper

10 What did Dewi find strange about the Cutter?

A. Such a small object could help him achieve greatness.

B. It felt strong but was actually useless.

C. Such a small object would easily be noticed by the noise it made.

D. The object was useful in some ways but not what he needed it for.

SECTION 2 – LINKED WORDS

Select the word from the options that fits best with the words in both sets of brackets.

11 (heal, medical) (search, find)

A. cure	B. recover	C. support	D. team	E. torch

12 (seek, talk) (method, manner)

A. hunt	B. counsel	C. solution	D. answer	E. approach

13 (body, vital) (moment, speed)

A. health	B. important	C. flash	D. heartbeat	E. second

14 (glue, connect) (relate, friend)

A. bond	B. stick	C. joined	D. comrade	E. ally

15 (restless, nervous) (music, strings)

A. tireless	B. bored	C. violin	D. fiddle	E. strum

SECTION 3 – COMPOUND WORDS

Underline a word from each set of brackets to make a new compound word.

16	(eye, see, look)	(frames, glasses, discs)
17	(finger, special, odd)	(tips, looking, showing)
18	(suffocate, choke, cough)	(grasp, hold, grip)
19	(up, top, peak)	(correct, left, right)
20	(smash, cracked, break)	(through, forward, progress)

SECTION 4 – ODD WORD OUT

Select the odd word out in each set of words.

21	A. captive	B. restrained	C. liberated	D. imprisoned
22	A. reject	B. dismiss	C. rebuff	D. conclude
23	A. smile	B. leer	C. smirk	D. grimace
24	A. complement	B. augment	C. enhance	D. contrast
25	A. pliant	B. firm	C. rigid	D. inflexible

SECTION 5 – ANAGRAMS

Rearrange the letters of the word on the left to make a suitable word for the sentence on the right.

26	BLEATS	The horse is resting in the [ ][ ][ ][ ][ ][ ].
27	HATRED	There isn't even a [ ][ ][ ][ ][ ][ ] of evidence to support your claim.
28	ITSELF	[ ][ ][ ][ ][ ][ ] your laughter lest you wish to offend him.
29	REACTS	This restaurant [ ][ ][ ][ ][ ][ ] to a wide variety of clientele.
30	SPREAD	She quickly [ ][ ][ ][ ][ ][ ] a shawl around her shoulders.

11 WORKSHEET

SECTION 1 – ADJECTIVES

Select the noun from the options provided that goes best with the adjective in **bold**.

1 **rational**

A. drawings	B. ideas	C. charts	D. quotes

2 **incoherent**

A. music	B. art	C. walk	D. speech

3 **inconsolable**

A. sobs	B. happiness	C. laughter	D. melodies

4 **incessant**

A. people	B. chatter	C. laziness	D. animals

5 **persistent**

A. fate	B. leave	C. yap	D. measure

SECTION 2 – SPELLING ERRORS

Select the word in each group that has not been spelled correctly.

6	A. involuntary	B. instananous	C. insubordinate	D. inscrutable	E. insignificant
7	A. spasmodic	B. spurning	C. serruptitious	D. separate	E. specialised
8	A. emulation	B. emancipation	C. emotional	D. emerging	E. emphattic
9	A. wrenching	B. wrangler	C. wrongful	D. worrysome	E. worrying
10	A. haphazerdly	B. hopeful	C. helpful	D. heartily	E. heatedly

SECTION 3 – WORD DEFINITIONS

Select the word that best matches the definition.

11 a sudden forward attacking motion

A. lurch	B. creep	C. prance	D. lunge

12 done without conscious effort

A. deliberate	B. involuntary	C. hesitantly	D. cautiously

13 appearing to have not been planned or organised

A. haphazard	B. dishevelled	C. fate	D. articulated

14 being very cruel and savage in nature

A. unsophisticated	B. criminal	C. barbaric	D. heretic

15 to cry intensely for a long period of time

A. whimper	B. scream	C. laugh	D. squall

SECTION 4 – PARTIAL SYNONYMS

Complete the words on the right to form a word that means the same or nearly the same as the word on the left.

16	HOLLER	S H _ _ _ K
17	INCONSOLABLE	H E _ _ _ B R O _ _ N
18	EMULATE	M I _ _ C
19	HAPHAZARDLY	A _ _ _ T R _ _ I L Y
20	BARBARIC	B R _ _ _ L

SECTION 1 – COMPREHENSION

Read the passage and answer the questions that follow.

an extract from *The Cadwaladr Quests – Tangled Time* – Chapter 12. **Trust**

As Drane lay nursing his battered leg on the office floor, on the other side of the door, in the exhibition hall, the Master continued to **goad** and taunt his old **adversary** Gwilym.

'What exactly are you going to do to stop me?' cackled Dewi, his eyes lit with raw threat; they exposed the **empathy** of a shark. 'How are you going to save your precious gem?' he mocked, spitting his words at Gwilym.

Gwilym didn't blink; his gaze rested **defiantly** on Dewi.

'The **devout** and everlasting knight. The **perpetual** hero. Underneath, you always were an **insipid** fool,' Dewi **ridiculed**. 'A slave to your people and **morality**, and where has it got you?' he hissed.

Not **retaliating**, Gwilym remained silent. His **stance** exhibited neither threat nor **provocation**. He simply stared at Dewi's dead expression.

'What is it, old man? Are you too scared to take me on?' **rasped** Dewi's **vengeful** voice, his **repressed** rage **erupting** in response to Gwilym's grace and **composure**. As he exploded, his fine features **contorted** to bare his **immoral soul**, that of a madman. 'You can't stop me, and you won't!' he screamed, aiming another stomach-**churning** blow at the case with the Cutter.

It shuddered and groaned. Smoke poured out, but its previous soft gold colour had now turned an ominous black. **Fiery** sparks flickered as the smoke **spewed**. The sweet smell of flowers had vanished, replaced by an **acrid**, sickening burning. Dewi's victory was surely near; a third strike to the case might finish it. Snarling, with a **demented** and **outlandish** twist of his face, he stretched his arm upwards as if reaching for the ceiling; then, he crashed it down with such forcible might that a **hideous, unearthly** vibration rang around the **capacious** hall. Delicate cracks emerged, **rifts** running in random branches throughout the glass, forming a complex network of venous tracks. Dewi snorted, licking his lips as he **hacked** the case with the Cutter again.

'Gwilym, stop him! Stop him!' shouted Claire, running from the office. 'Don't just stand there!'

1 Select a word in the first five lines that tells us that the Master was trying to provoke Gwilym.

A. 'adversary'

B. 'threat'

C. 'mocked'

D. 'goad'

2 What about Gwilym's body language shows us that he was unafraid?

A. He stared at Dewi with unblinking defiance.

B. He recited the Knight's Code of Chivalry.

C. He told Dewi his plan.

D. He pushed Dewi out of the way.

3 How can we sum up Dewi's opinion of Gwilym?

A. Dewi thinks Gwilym is quite unintelligent and boring.

B. Dewi thinks Gwilym is dully heroic and clings unnecessarily to old morals.

C. Dewi thinks Gwilym is admirable and heroic.

D. Dewi thinks Gwilym is two-faced and hiding something.

4 What was Gwilym's response to Dewi's taunting?

A. Gwilym responded by rushing at Dewi.

B. Gwilym responded by remaining still.

C. Gwilym responded by taunting Dewi.

D. Gwilym responded by giving a battle cry.

5 Which word in lines 10 to 15 tells us what Dewi's voice sounds like?

A. 'repressed'

B. 'immoral'

C. 'erupting'

D. 'rasped'

6 Which colloquial phrase from the passage means the same as 'fight me'?

A. 'What is it, old man?'

B. 'take me on'

C. 'can't stop me'

D. 'Don't just stand there!'

7 Why was Dewi so enraged?

A. He was angry at Claire.

B. He was angry at Jack for attacking Drane.

C. He had lost the Gwalch Gem.

D. He was not getting the response he wanted from Gwilym.

8 How did the smell in the room change?

A. It changed from a flowery smell to an acrid stench.

B. It changed from a soapy smell to and acrid stench.

C. It changed from an acrid stench to a flowery smell.

D. It changed from an acrid stench to a soapy smell.

9 Which word in lines 15 to 20 suggests the certainty of Dewi's victory?

A. 'ominous'

B. 'surely'

C. 'outlandish'

D. 'unearthly'

10 Which two words tell us that things are not normal?

A. 'contorted' and 'immoral'

B. 'immoral' and 'outlandish'

C. 'outlandish' and 'unearthly'

D. 'unearthly' and 'capacious'

SECTION 2 – CHANGE ONE LETTER

Change just one letter in the word on the left to create a new word that matches the description given.

11	OUTRACED	angered or offended by something	________
12	WILTED	rejected by someone	________
13	LIPID	enraged	________
14	PLANT	to lean noticeably	________
15	SLEETING	for a moment	________

SECTION 3 – PARTIAL WORDS

Work out the missing letters to complete the word – a definition of each word is given.

16	C _ N C _ _ T	to devise or fabricate a story or plan
17	U _ _ _ R S _ _ T _ D	modest and sensible
18	G _ R _ E _ _ S	of great beauty
19	I N _ _ L _ R _ _ _ E	unbearably difficult to deal with
20	P _ _ _ U _ E	plentiful

SECTION 4 – CLOZE

Choose the correct words from the table to fill in the gaps in the text.

A	B	C	D	E
onslaught	premonition	withheld	miraculously	quashed

21 ________, the case had **22** ________ Dewi's **23** ________ with the Cutter, and the bracelet had survived unharmed, lying before her in the case. But this joy was **24** ________ by the vision she had just seen. Had it been an omen, or even worse, a **25** ________?

SECTION 5 – SPELLING ERRORS

Select the word in each group that has not been spelled correctly.

26	A. evidently	B. analyse	C. irreparably	D. immorale	E. vengeful
27	A. perpetual	B. outlandish	C. demented	D. unearthly	E. capatious
28	A. hubristically	B. ferosious	C. lamented	D. bolstered	E. bemused
29	A. mesmersie	B. remnant	C. onslaught	D. concisely	E. miraculously
30	A. hapless	B. mirthful	C. fortutous	D. constituent	E. agitated

13 WORKSHEET

SECTION 1 – LINKED WORDS

Select the word from the options that fits best with the words in both sets of brackets.

1 (aroma, perfume) (plants, gift)

A. scent	B. odour	C. flower	D. bouquet	E. bunch

2 (effect, impression) (postage, letter)

A. mark	B. stamp	C. indent	D. document	E. paper

3 (residence, street) (speech, greeting)

A. address	B. road	C. abode	D. salute	E. announce

4 (fun, enjoyment) (event, dance)

A. glee	B. play	C. masquerade	D. sport	E. ball

5 (fright, pale) (boil, scald)

A. shock	B. whiten	C. simmer	D. water	E. blanch

SECTION 2 – CLOZE

Choose the correct words from the table to fill in the gaps in the text.

A	B	C	D	E
fissure	crinkle	languid	precision	swirled

As the two knights left the museum, a faint **6** __________ of an echo followed them, its cheerful, melodic notes drifting in waves across the empty hall, akin to wind chimes tinkling in unison as if pushed by a **7** __________ summer breeze. A smell of fresh lilies **8** __________ upwards, once again filling the air with sweet perfume. Then slowly, one by one, every crack, every split, every **9** __________ in the glass case retraced its original tracks with pinpoint mathematical **10** __________, until there were none.

SECTION 3 – SHUFFLED SENTENCES

Use the following words, except for one, to make complete sentences. Underline the word that is not used.

11 through rode the his the countryside middle motorbike renegade

12 plummeted melting temperature the knew before we even

13 ineptitude is your starting really are me annoy to

14 dishes and away wash stop your those larking now

15 dinner for was I to have what ponder wondering

SECTION 4 – SYNONYMS

Select the word from the options that is closest in meaning to the word in **bold** on the left.

16	**disgraced**	A. despised	B. besmirched	C. reviled	D. disgusted
17	**reiterated**	A. repeated	B. rewarded	C. responded	D. reimbursed
18	**decoy**	A. theft	B. description	C. diversion	D. appraisement
19	**officious**	A. boring	B. deceptive	C. unpleasant	D. domineering
20	**clarify**	A. inspire	B. unravel	C. transpose	D. invigorate

14 WORKSHEET

SECTION 1 – COMPREHENSION

Read the passage and answer the questions that follow.

an extract from The Cadwaladr Quests – Tangled Time – Chapter 14. **Luxury in Defeat**

Outside the museum, Claire didn't see the **chauffeur**-driven black Bentley glide past them; she was too busy strapping herself into the front of Jayne's smart four-wheel drive. As her seat belt connected and she glanced outside, she narrowly missed the handsome, stylishly attired man in the back, who scrutinised her through the tinted window. He had **misjudged** her; he wouldn't make that mistake twice.

He rolled a matchstick-sized object in one hand and held an **oblong** metal box in the other. Fascinated, he studied the Cutter between his fingers. Why had it failed him? Why had the glass not succumbed to its targeted blows? What had that **shrewd**, **sly** little knight Evans done to it?

Curious, he checked it from all angles, observing its plain yet **bewitching** form. His eyes flashed but his face matched that of stone. Only the rhythmic tapping of his foot, like the swish of a cat's vexed tail, hinted at his seething irritation. The Knights Hawk had won this round. A seasoned businessman, he'd lost deals before but always found other ways to win. **Resilience** and, of course, **ruthlessness** were the key to success. He had plenty of both.

Holding the unique object with care, he laid it back in the purpose-built box. He paused, before closing the lid and tucking it into the breast pocket of his Savile Row suit.

His long, manicured nail tapped on the opaque glass that separated him from the front. His tap turned the screen **transparent**, revealing his female driver. Catching her eye in the rear-view mirror, he nodded once, then tapped the screen again, returning it to **privacy** mode, then **reclined** into the **decadent opulence** of **plush** cream leather. He directed his eyes up towards the **extravagant** vehicle's leather-trimmed roof and **gesticulated** his hand in a dismissive wave. A screen made from ultra-thin graphene glided down, halting at eye level. **Columns** of rapid figures flickered, shifting from red to green then back to red again. His intelligent eyes scanned the ever-changing columns of numbers. He absorbed the fast-changing digits, computing each meaningful and **consequential** detail with ease. He swiped at the air with his finger, flipping the view. More rows flickered in different **time zones**; his gaze followed the **erratic** changes of this morning's **financial** markets. Satisfied, he gestured again, and the graphene screen retracted.

It would be a long journey, time to **ponder** his next move. He signalled into the air again. The **rapturous** piano notes of Rachmaninoff's **Concerto** Number Two in C **Minor filtered** with unobtrusive clarity into the Bentley's **ostentatious** back seat. The sound quality **sublime** and **orchestral**.

Goosebumps prickled his arms. Rarely affected by emotions, he was moved by this music. He **unwound**, resting his head back and inhaling the fine-smelling leather of his **exorbitant** yet tasteful **customised** car. *I must allow more **leisure** time*, he **reprimanded** himself. *Perhaps a **yacht***, he thought.

He lifted a heavy glass up towards the light, inspecting the rising **amber** bubbles. He popped his minute **thermometer** into the top of his champagne **flute**. The digital reader displayed the **extortionate beverage's** exact temperature.

Obsessive attention to detail was one of his key **attributes**; he prided himself on precision and accuracy – some have even called him **eccentric**. Smiling, he loosened his tie and savoured a **liberal** sip of perfectly chilled **vintage** champagne. Uninterrupted and absorbing the divine music, he quashed his anger, closed his eyes and enjoyed the **luxurious** ride home.

1 **Why is a hyphen used between the words 'chauffeur' and 'driven' (line 1)?**

A. It tells us to pause.

B. It breaks up two clauses.

C. It forms a compound modifier that tells us that the car was driven by a chauffeur.

D. It adds an explanation.

2 **What was strange about the Cutter?**

A. It could cut through anything.

B. It had a plain form but was captivating to look at.

C. It had runes written on it.

D. It appeared to be able to unlock something important.

3 **How did the Master turn the screen transparent?**

A. He swiped across it.

B. He knocked on it.

C. He used a scanner.

D. He tapped on it.

4 **Select the correct combination of words used to emphasise the Master's wealth.**

A. 'manicured'; 'decadent'; 'erratic'

B. 'decadent'; 'opulence'; 'financial'

C. 'decadent'; 'opulence'; 'plush'

D. 'consequential'; 'financial'; 'rapturous'

5 **What activity did the Master partake in that involved graphs and figures?**

A. dabbling in the financial markets

B. taking stock of expenses

C. prioritising his agenda

D. doing complex mathematical calculations

6 **What did the Master plan to do with the time the journey would take?**

A. He would study a new subject.

B. He would contemplate his course of action.

C. He would compose a musical piece.

D. He would read some books.

7 **What does the use of the word 'unobtrusive' (line 27) tell us about the way the music sounded?**

A. It was loud and raucous.

B. It was barely audible.

C. It was set to an audible level that would not cause any distraction.

D. There was a problem with the speakers, and they distorted the sound.

8 Find a word in the last three paragraphs that tells us that the car was modified specifically for the Master.

A. 'exorbitant'

B. 'customised'

C. 'extortionate'

D. 'obsessive'

9 How is the Master's excessive attention to detail highlighted when he drank?

A. He carefully measured each sip.

B. He poured an exact amount of liquid into the glass.

C. He made sure his drink was exactly the right temperature.

D. He counted the number of bubbles in his drink.

10 Select the best description for the Master's personality as shown in this chapter.

A. obstreperous and quick to anger

B. patient and passive

C. impulsive and hot-headed

D. meticulous and goal-oriented

SECTION 2 – CLOZE

Choose the word that best completes the sentence.

11 The __________ display impressed the audience greatly.

A. modest

B. ostentatious

C. presumptuous

D. ostensible

12 He liked to __________ on Saturdays by doing a bit of gardening.

A. unleash

B. unhinge

C. unfurl

D. unwind

13 You can __________ your home to suit your lifestyle.

A. customise

B. grow

C. keep

D. control

14 She was considered quite __________ for her odd mannerisms and fashion sense.

A. excessive

B. exorbitant

C. eccentric

D. ecclesiastic

15 The dog stretched itself out on the __________ wool carpeting.

A. luxurious

B. lucky

C. luminous

D. lupine

SECTION 3 – WORD DEFINITIONS

Select the definition that best matches the word.

A. to come to the wrong conclusion
B. to tell only half the truth
C. to be openly hostile
D. displaying a keen sense of judgement
E. a method of transportation
F. someone who is hired to drive a private car
G. to anger someone
H. to tempt someone into making a bad decision
I. to give in to pressure or negative influences
J. a small mouse-like rodent

16	chauffeur	______
17	misjudge	______
18	succumb	______
19	shrewd	______
20	vex	______

SECTION 4 – PARTIAL ANTONYMS

Complete the antonym of the word on the left.

21	cheap	E X _ _ A _ A _ _ N T
22	liberal	M E _ S _ Y
23	consistent	E R _ A _ _ C
24	row	C _ L _ _ N
25	modest	O S _ E N _ A T _ _ _ S

SECTION 5 – RHYMING

Find a word that rhymes with the word on the left to complete the sentence.

26	RECLINED	The cashier D E _ _ _ _ _ _ to take cash at the counter.
27	LEISURE	He took great P _ _ A _ _ _ E in pushing her into the fountain.
28	RUDE	The man in the suit has S H _ _ _ D business sense.
29	VEXED	The dog was P E _ _ L _ _ E D upon looking in the mirror.
30	PONDERED	She W _ _ D _ _ E D into the woods.

SECTION 1 – MISSING LETTERS

Find the three letters that have been removed from the word in CAPITALS. Once these letters are placed back in the word, the sentence will make sense.

1 He admitted GRINGLY to actually enjoying the meal.

A. udg	B. edg	C. edi	D. udi

2 There was an AARD silence following her announcement.

A. ekw	B. wkg	C. wkw	D. dkw

3 He could tell she wasn't being sincere by the SONIC tone of her voice.

A. art	B. are	C. arb	D. ard

4 He was great at DIPLCY, even though he wasn't sociable.

A. oma	B. uma	C. ima	D. ema

5 She couldn't help feeling DETED after the argument with her mother.

A. dec	B. sec	C. jec	D. tec

SECTION 2 – JUMBLED PARAGRAPHS

Choose the most logical order of sentences to construct a meaningful paragraph.

6
a) Claire likes to wear garish clothes.
b) Her friend Imelda prefers a more conservative wardrobe.
c) Unlike Claire, Imelda feels that appearance should be second to personality.
d) She likes to see the reaction that she gets from strangers.

A. a d b c	B. d a c b	C. b d c a	D. c b a d

7
a) It might be fun to see things from their perspective sometimes.
b) They actively seek out the most daring adventures.
c) Fortunately, they often have a group of like-minded individuals for support.
d) It seems that some people are inherently attracted to danger.

A. a b d c	B. d c a b	C. d b a c	D. a b c d

8 a) Always consult a guidebook or expert if you are unsure.

b) There are certain traits that help to identify poisonous mushrooms.

c) When foraging, it should be noted that certain mushrooms are inedible.

d) While not all of them are deadly, a number of them are harmful.

A. a b d c	B. d c a b	C. c d b a	D. a b c d

9 a) The company decided not to prolong the inevitable any longer.

b) They cited a steady profit loss as their motivation.

c) They gave their staff notice that the company would be closing.

d) Eventually, shares were sold off at low rates.

A. d a d c	B. d c a b	C. b d c a	D. a c b d

10 a) He managed to accumulate a lot of money by saving a little bit at a time.

b) Dad is always looking for the next bargain.

c) He always used to say, 'Never pay full price for something.'

d) Now I apply the same mentality when buying certain things.

A. b a c d	B. d c b a	C. b d a c	D. c a b d

SECTION 3 – VOCABULARY IN CONTEXT

Select the most appropriate option that matches the meaning of the word <u>underlined</u> in the sentence.

11 Claire, sighing with exhaustion and relief, melted into the <u>sumptuous</u> front passenger seat of Jayne's car.

A. The front seat was filled with food.

B. Claire evaporated into the seat.

C. The seat was large and comfortable.

D. The front seat was heated.

E. Claire was very tired and hungry.

12 The spacious interior smelled of leather and Jayne's <u>arresting</u> yet irresistible perfume.

A. Jayne's perfume was very noticeable.

B. The police were waiting to arrest Jayne.

C. Jayne was an undercover police agent.

D. Perfume had been spilled.

E. The leather was scented with perfume.

13 Claire was used to squashing into her mum's battered old banger.

A. Claire's mum often made bangers and mash.
B. Claire's mum's car was old, damaged and noisy.
C. Claire's mum had a small car.
D. Their car had junk rolling around inside, making a noise.
E. Their car was a vintage model.

14 Her mum drove her mad sometimes, yet Claire realised how tough juggling three kids and a full-time job must be as a single parent.

A. Claire's mum was a trained circus performer.
B. Claire's mother had to take her kids with her to work.
C. Claire had to look after her siblings while her mother worked.
D. Claire was responsible for helping her mother organise her schedule.
E. Claire's mum had to balance raising her kids with going to work.

15 Dee's own childhood had been dire, and she had always vowed not to repeat the same mistakes, no matter how dreadful things got for her.

A. Dee had a sheltered childhood.
B. Dee wanted the same type of childhood for her children.
C. Dee had a problematic childhood.
D. Dee was neglectful as a parent.
E. Dee had a wonderful childhood.

SECTION 4 – ODD WORD OUT

Select the odd word out in each set of words.

16	A. compliment	B. accolade	C. judgement	D. admiration
17	A. accept	B. baulk	C. anticipate	D. enjoy
18	A. withered	B. dehydrated	C. parched	D. drenched
19	A. lowered	B. vociferous	C. hushed	D. still
20	A. cheerful	B. exuberant	C. elated	D. crestfallen

16 WORKSHEET

SECTION 1 – COMPREHENSION

Read the passage and answer the questions that follow.

an extract from The Cadwaladr Quests – Tangled Time – Chapter 16. **Finding Gladys**

Gladys fell silent, a **pensive** look on her face.

Claire cringed again, mortified at her **rude** comment. She mentally **scolded** herself; Evans was a Knight Hawk, after all. However, if she was being honest, she didn't like the way he made her feel. The ensuing painful silence from Gladys proved ample punishment for her lack of tact.

'Did you say Robert Evans was on the train with you earlier?' Gladys eventually asked in a quiet voice.

'Yes, he was. After seeing him today when we arrived through that awful tunnel, I assumed you or Gwilym had sent him,' answered Claire, relieved that Gladys hadn't told her off for her comment, or, being **diplomatic**, had seemingly **sidestepped** it.

'So there are two bits to the Cutter, then?' continued Claire, trying to fill the awkward silence.

'Yes. The Knights Hawk sealed the Gwalch Gem bracelet in the case. The glass is impenetrable unless both parts of the Cutter are used to open it. Two tiny, identical arrows. Alone they are useless; together they are all-powerful. Today Dewi discovered more to the gem's security than he realised.'

Claire massaged Jack's ear again. 'So if Dewi has half of the Cutter, Mr Evans has the other?' asked Claire.

'Yes, Robert Evans has it. Today at the museum, Evans recognised Drane's **accomplished** Mal-Instinctive power and knew the Master was close. Evans acted without hesitation to save the Gwalch Gem bracelet.'

'Accomplished? Rat-Boy Drane? He can't be that great if I managed to beat him.'

'Maybe it says more about you than you realise,' Gladys replied.

Claire felt a huge rush of pride and couldn't disguise her grin at the thought of what she'd done.

'Where's Mr Evans now, then?'

Gladys hesitated. 'We're not **entirely** certain.'

'What do you mean, you're not certain? You're ***never*** not certain about anything, Gladys!'

Gladys got up and took a cloth from the sink and mopped the tea splashes from the worn **vinyl** tablecloth.

'There are far-reaching tunnels that run from the edges of the museum's basement and beyond. They are most complicated, intertwining and **unforgiving**. No Mal-Instinctive knows them as well as they would like. They are **primarily** Evans's work, and he **traverses** them better than any other knight.'

'Gosh,' said Claire. Maybe she *had* underestimated Evans.

'Evans escaped with one arrow before Dewi reached him. He left the other for Dewi to find, to throw him off the trail. Dewi thought he had the whole Cutter until it failed to break through the glass, but we are still waiting to hear from Evans,' she finished.

'Is that unusual?' asked Claire. 'Should you have heard from him by now?'

'Possibly, although not necessarily.'

'Why *was* he on the train with me this morning?' Claire asked, but Gladys didn't answer.

'I suspect you are wondering what happens now, cariad.'

'Yes,' Claire blurted. 'Yes, I am.'

Gladys smiled a weary smile and said, 'You have no **obligation** to us; everything you pursue is your choice, and always has been.'

'Yes,' Claire mouthed in a half whisper. 'Yes, I suppose it is,' she finished, expecting her future would prove more complicated than she'd anticipated.

'It's getting late. You mustn't put your mum through any more **heartache**; she has suffered enough for one day.'

'Gosh, yes. Is that the time?' She plopped Jack down from her lap and kissed his head. 'See you Monday, **buddy**.'

1 How do we know that Gladys was deep in thought?

A. She had a pensive look on her face.

B. She spoke with a soft voice.

C. She tried to think carefully about her words.

D. She wanted to have time alone to think.

2 What is meant when it says that Claire was 'mortified' (line 2)?

A. She was in the process of dying.

B. She was suffering from arthritis.

C. She was very scared.

D. She was greatly embarrassed.

3 Find the adjective in the first ten lines that means 'showing tact'.

A. 'mentally'

B. 'ensuing'

C. 'diplomatic'

D. 'seemingly'

4 Identify the word in the first fifteen lines that can be used for both a physical movement and a conversational tactic.

A. 'cringed'

B. 'lack'

C. 'sidestepped'

D. 'accomplished'

5 What security measure was in place to protect the Gwalch Gem bracelet?

A. The glass case would only open if the correct password was used.

B. The glass case would only open if both parts of the Cutter were used.

C. The gem would only respond to the right person.

D. The gem was placed in a reinforced steel vault.

6 'Rat-Boy' (line 17) is an example of ...

A. a simile

B. a metaphor

C. a hyphenated compound noun

D. a short-form adjective

7 Find an example of a double negative in lines 20 to 40.

A. 'never not'

B. 'far-reaching'

C. 'not necessarily'

D. 'no obligation'

8 Why is Evans able to navigate the tunnels so well?

A. He has a tracking dog.

B. He is naturally gifted at tracking.

C. He is responsible for creating most of the tunnels.

D. He has a map.

9 What does Claire's mouthing in a 'half whisper' (line 39) tell us about her feelings?

A. She was confused.

B. She was scared.

C. She was coming to a realisation.

D. She was having some doubt.

10 Rephrase 'everything you pursue is your choice' (lines 37–38).

A. 'Your fate is out of your hands.'

B. 'Be careful of your choices.'

C. 'All you wish for will come true.'

D. 'You have free will.'

SECTION 2 – SPELLING ERRORS

Select the word in each group that has not been spelled correctly.

11	A. hospitable	B. hostility	C. hospice	D. hospital	E. hospitilaty
12	A. texture	B. textile	C. treck	D. traverse	E. contextual
13	A. ludicrous	B. lugubruous	C. legibility	D. leviable	E. lenient
14	A. inseperable	B. insufferable	C. inscrutable	D. inevitable	E. inedible
15	A. crockery	B. clutter	C. cringe	D. clamor	E. classicist

SECTION 3 – WORD DEFINITIONS

Select the most appropriate definition for each word highlighted in **bold**.

Gladys fell silent, a **pensive** look on her face.

Claire cringed again, **mortified** at her rude comment. She mentally **scolded** herself; Evans was a Knight Hawk, after all. However, if she was being honest, she didn't like the way he made her feel. The **ensuing** painful silence from Gladys proved **ample** punishment for her lack of tact.

16	reflective or meditative	______________
17	reprimanded someone	______________
18	enough or plentiful	______________
19	greatly ashamed	______________
20	following	______________

SECTION 4 – SHUFFLED SENTENCES

Rearrange the words to form a meaningful sentence and find the superfluous word.

21 records watches he to in time collect likes his free vinyl

22 but desert the to patient unforgiving the climate toughest is all

23 the extraction the oil crude of on primarily focuses rig company

24 they in compose the barren to a traverse had wagon wastelands

25 feel a obligation I unsavoury with no negotiate characters absolutely to

SECTION 5 – PARTIAL SYNONYMS

Select the correct combination of letters to complete the synonym of the word on the left.

26 maybe: _ e r h _ _ s

A. per	B. pre	C. pap	D. cap

27 mucky: s _ i _ e _

A. old	B. eld	C. ole	D. ins

28 skywards: h _ a _ e _ w a r d s

A. evd	B. evs	C. evq	D. evn

29 altitude: _ l e _ a t i _ n

A. eva	B. eve	C. evo	D. evu

30 steady: b _ l a _ c e _

A. ask	B. apt	C. and	D. aft

SECTION 1 – ADJECTIVES

Select the noun from the options that most closely relates to the adjective in **bold**.

1	woollen	A. shoes	B. sweater	C. purse	D. belt
2	medieval	A. current	B. times	C. modern	D. renaissance
3	perilous	A. journey	B. trade	C. embark	D. vacation
4	unaided	A. exasperation	B. mission	C. check	D. deviation
5	untested	A. accusation	B. feat	C. requirement	D. theory

SECTION 2 – HOMOPHONES

Select the most appropriate answer from the options available.

6 He'll ________ his eyes out when he finds out he's not ________ to go to the party.

A. ball, aloud
B. bawl, aloud
C. ball, allowed
D. bawl, allowed

7 The ________ tree was ________ in the winter.

A. beach, bare
B. beech, bare
C. beach, bear
D. beech, bear

8 She couldn't ________ the subject while picking a dress at the ________ shop.

A. broach, bridle
B. brooch, bridal
C. broach, bridal
D. brooch, bridle

9 ________ turn is it to ride the ________?

A. Who's, sleigh
B. Who's, slay
C. Whose, sleigh
D. Whose, slay

10 We will have __________ for the starter and the __________ for dessert.

A. muscles, moose

B. muscles, mousse

C. mussels, moose

D. mussels, mousse

SECTION 3 – LINKED WORDS

Select the word from the options that fits best with the words in both sets of brackets.

11 (impede, obstruct) (basket, container)

A. stop	B. hinder	C. hamper	D. box	E. bag

12 (water, drought) (desire, ambition)

A. rain	B. flood	C. wish	D. motivation	E. thirst

13 (take-off, aeroplane) (corridor, staircase)

A. landing	B. bedroom	C. helicopter	D. kitchen	E. taxi

14 (subterranean, underneath) (hidden, secret)

A. cavernous	B. lower	C. concealed	D. underground	E. beneath

15 (bad, malodorous) (pollute, stain)

A. nasty	B. smelly	C. chicken	D. bird	E. foul

SECTION 4 – CLOZE

Read through the text and use the words in **bold** to fill in the gaps in the sentences that follow.

As she stepped over the threshold back into the cavernous Via-Corp headquarters, displaying no contrition, Jayne Lewis wasted not a single thought on the subordinate, puny man she left on the floor.

16	He was feeling a sense of __________ after reprimanding his daughter for leaving her toys out.
17	She looked at the __________ boy with contempt, as she felt superior to him.
18	There is an old myth that vampires cannot cross a __________ unless invited in.
19	They stepped into the __________ lair cautiously, not wanting to awaken any bats.
20	He spoke to his __________ with respect, as he knew that everyone has to start somewhere.

WORKSHEET 18

SECTION 1 – COMPREHENSION

Read the passage and answer the questions that follow.

an extract from *The Cadwaladr Quests – Tangled Time* – Chapter 18. **A Silent Witness**

No one came. No knight in shining armour materialised, no rufty-tufty Jack Russell or smiling octogenarian appeared. A huge wave of disappointment, almost **grief**, washed over Claire, and any **semblance** of hope was swept clean away.

Jayne was in the process of stealing the Gwalch Gem bracelet from the glass case. This meant only one thing: she must have both halves of the Cutter, the only tool capable of fracturing the magical glass.

Claire's mind raced. How had this traitorous **impostor** managed to do this? Claire knew the Master had escaped with one half of the Cutter, and Gladys had said the knight Evans had taken the other half away to safety. Claire had never trusted Robert Evans.

Her heart was beating in her throat as she saw several things simultaneously: her once-beloved Jayne plucking the Gwalch Gem bracelet from the case and slipping it **ceremoniously** onto her wrist as a crumpled Marjorie Evans appeared from the shadows behind, handing something to Jayne. Claire squinted to make out the object and realised the birdlike Mrs Evans was handing her school bag to Jayne. Claire had left it at the museum earlier. Then, without a word, Jayne took the bag and pirouetted in her ballet shoes, leaving the building, making no more noise than a shadow.

Claire felt like she'd swallowed a bag of snakes. Stricken by the **injustice** of Jayne's deceit, she knew if she tried to move, she would sob out loud and give herself away.

Powerless, Claire lay on her side as hot, silent tears sploshed down her face, trickling off the end of her nose onto the floor. A blanket of despair smothered her. Unable to collect herself, she pulled up her hood and snuggled hopelessly into the fur trim that surrounded her wet face.

Transient shadows scattered **hither** and **thither**, ducking back and forth, hiding amidst a thick murk of fog. Unsure of how long she had lain there, minutes or hours, Claire blinked furiously, urging her eyes to focus. A shard of stark, bright light shone in a horizontal strip to her right whilst a soft orange haze glowed down to her left. Then she remembered. The horror of Jayne's vile betrayal surfaced like a waking monster. She had lain so still, in such comatose desolation, she must have dozed off.

Sitting up slowly as her eyes adjusted to the light, she was struck by something oddly familiar. The outlines and **silhouettes** in the room now comprised shapes she recognised well. Instinctively fumbling to her right, she found the switch and turned on the lamp. She lay in bed, her own bed, in her room, at home.

Reeling, she snatched at her **duvet** and threw it off. She was wearing her pyjamas; they had stuck to her skin, soaked and cooling rapidly to a chilly sog. She shivered. She'd experienced this feeling before but never so strong as now. Waking from a dream so vivid, so palpably real, for several confused seconds, she had almost believed it was happening. The immense relief hit her so hard she laughed out loud.

'I knew it!' she said. 'I knew it! Jayne would never do that to me,' she laughed.

When her heart had slowed and some semblance of calm had worked its way through her, she hopped out of bed and quickly changed her pyjamas. On her chest of drawers, Wallace's head lay next to Gromit, but now the clock was ticking again. She picked it up and put it to her ear, listening to the rhythmic tick-tock. The clock said 3.30 a.m.

Having no idea whether it showed the right time, she crawled back into bed. As she was wide awake now, she leaned across and grabbed her book from her bedside table and read a few pages. But the words refused to **register**, and after repeatedly reading the same sentence over and over, she gave up and returned to where she had started, re-creasing the triangle at the top corner of the page.

Putting down her book, leaving her lamp on, she closed her eyes, but her mind tormented her, insisting on revisiting the nightmare she had just woken from. It had been so graphic.

1 What is an 'octogenarian' (line 1)?

A. a person who studies octopuses

B. someone who draws eight-sided shapes

C. a person in their eighties

D. someone who only eats octopus

2 What is suggested about Jayne when she was stealing the Gwalch Gem bracelet?

A. It is suggested she was using magic.

B. It is suggested she had both halves of the Cutter.

C. It is suggested the Gwalch Gem would respond to her.

D. It is suggested she had stealth on her side.

3 What word is used in lines 6 to 11 to tell us Claire's mental state?

A. 'raced'

B. 'traitorous'

C. 'beating'

D. 'crumpled'

4 What does the use of the word 'ceremoniously' (line 10) tell us about Jayne's regard of the bracelet?

A. Jayne has no regard for it.

B. Jayne holds it in high regard.

C. Jayne prefers not to think about it.

D. Jayne tries not to give it too much reverence.

5 How does the simile about snakes bring attention to Claire's feelings (line 15)?

A. It tells us how much she hates snakes.

B. It tells us how betrayed she feels.

C. It tells us how sick Claire is.

D. It tells us about Claire's interest in snakes.

6 What phrasal verb is used to tell us that Claire fell asleep?

A. 'to focus'

B. 'down to'

C. 'dozed off'

D. 'sitting up'

7 What emotion did Claire experience after she was woken up?

A. relief

B. confusion

C. mania

D. joy

8 What is meant when it says 'the words refused to register' (lines 38–39)?

A. Claire was unable to focus on what she was reading.

B. Claire was having problems with her vision.

C. Claire was having problems with her hearing.

D. Claire could not understand the meaning of the words.

9 What grammatical device is used to tell us that Claire had marked the page in the book more than once?

A. a conjunction

B. a semicolon

C. a prefix

D. a preposition

10 Find a word in the last paragraph that means 'realistic'.

A. 'discern'

B. 'tormented'

C. 'insisting'

D. 'graphic'

SECTION 2 – SPELLING ERRORS

Select the word in each group that has not been spelled correctly.

11	A. grievious	B. grieving	C. grinning	D. grinned	E. grief
12	A. semblence	B. sampled	C. assembled	D. resembled	E. somniferous
13	A. ceremony	B. ceremonously	C. cerebral	D. ceremonial	E. certificate
14	A. injustice	B. injurious	C. inconspicious	D. imposition	E. internment
15	A. transient	B. transition	C. transference	D. transitionary	E. transistory

SECTION 3 – ANAGRAMS

Rearrange the word on the left to form a new word that makes sense in the sentence on the right.

16	ALIGNED	They are the ☐☐☐☐☐☐☐ car brand on the market.
17	ASTRIDE	She was weary of his ☐☐☐☐☐☐☐ on taxes and the income gap.
18	STARRED	☐☐☐☐☐☐☐ are welcome to set up their stalls in the park on Saturday.
19	PIRATES	I used to go to ☐☐☐☐☐☐☐ when I was younger, but not any more.
20	ALLERGY	Her talent goes ☐☐☐☐☐☐☐ ignored by her superiors.

SECTION 4 – PARTIAL ANTONYMS

Complete the antonym of the word on the left.

21	ambiguously	E X _ _ I _ _ T _ _
22	cloak	R _ _ E _ L
23	permanent	T R _ _ S _ _ N _
24	obscene	D _ C _ _ T
25	desire	A _ A _ _ Y

SECTION 5 – WORD SWAP

Select the two words that need to swap places for the sentence to make sense.

	A	B	C	D	E	F	G	H
26	The	gem	bracelet's	completely	place	was	safe	deserted
27	Her	sun	was	scorched	by	the	blazing	skin
28	As	she	woke	Claire's	up	vision	was	unclear
29	She	was	a	this	witness	to	lone	crime
30	Her	delayed	limbs	were	numb	with	lower	shock

WORKSHEET 19

SECTION 1 – ANTONYM PAIRS

Which of the following pairs are NOT antonyms?

1
A. intervene, arbitrate
B. allow, forbid
C. celebrate, defame
D. partake, avoid
E. play, spectate

2
A. grand, minor
B. ulterior, overt
C. reminiscent, comparable
D. despicable, praiseworthy
E. debt, credit

3
A. beneficial, detrimental
B. obsequious, intimidating
C. common, rare
D. memorable, forgettable
E. undoubtedly, unquestionably

4
A. dwindle, wane
B. slacken, tighten
C. heedless, cautious
D. finicky, unfussy
E. subjective, impartial

5
A. malignant, benign
B. preamble, finale
C. giddy, balanced
D. attentive, preoccupied
E. slender, willowy

SECTION 2 – SYNONYMS

Select the word from the options that is closest in meaning to the word in **bold** on the left.

6	**portentous**	A. insignificant	B. petty	C. trivial	D. fateful
7	**vulnerable**	A. immune	B. defenceless	C. resilient	D. fortified
8	**shrill**	A. squawky	B. mellow	C. low	D. lilting
9	**amusement**	A. boredom	B. apathy	C. weariness	D. merriment
10	**snobby**	A. modest	B. pretentious	C. unassuming	D. humble

SECTION 3 – CLOZE

Choose the word that best completes the sentence.

11 They had let her __________ yesterday morning.

A. overburden	B. overwhelm	C. oversleep	D. overarch

12 Claire woke weighed down with a __________ sense of doom.

A. comical	B. vivid	C. creative	D. portentous

13 A silence fell as Claire and Pete __________ glances.

A. revived	B. exchanged	C. engaged	D. educated

14 Claire __________ out loud, hoping her mum hadn't heard.

A. laughed	B. reached	C. remembered	D. exhaled

15 'I need to __________ now though, if you don't mind,'

A. hurry	B. laugh	C. caution	D. hear

SECTION 4 – WORD DEFINITIONS

Select the correct definition for the given words.

16 'lingering'

A. disappearing quickly

B. staying for an extended period of time

C. appearing briefly

D. moving at a slow pace

17 'appalling'

A. appearing in a natural light

B. causing a person to run away

C. causing great shock or horror

D. giving a bad impression

18 'heft'

A. a thrown object

B. the force with which you run at something

C. the expense of something

D. the heaviness of someone or something

19 'laddie'

A. a young dog

B. a young boy

C. a young girl

D. a young bird

20 'quip'

A. a smart comment

B. a weapon for punishment

C. a harsh statement

D. a critique

20 WORKSHEET

SECTION 1 – COMPREHENSION

Read the passage and answer the questions that follow.

an extract from The Cadwaladr Quests – Tangled Time – Chapter 20. **An Unexpected Change of Plan**

'Claire, open this door now,' Dee hissed in a low, insistent voice.

'What is it? What's wrong, Mum? Becca's OK, isn't she?' asked Claire, opening the door, worried her sister might have been taken ill.

'Yes, yes, *she's* fine. It's me that's not! Your father has just knocked on the door unexpectedly, and I opened it to him dressed like this!' Dee groaned, pointing to her dressing gown.

'Mum, is that it? I thought something was *really* wrong. You're fine. Pink fluffy suits you,' she joked as she headed past Dee down the stairs.

Vince stood in their lounge, talking gaming **strategy** with Pete.

'Hiya, Dad. What is it?' Claire asked, that earlier niggle returning **with a vengeance**.

'Hi, darling. How are you today?' asked Vince, **pecking** her on the cheek before hugging her.

'I'm fine, Dad,' said Claire. 'Why are you here today? Is everything OK?'

'Yes, love, everything's fine. Did you sleep OK last night?' he asked.

Claire knew full well her dad didn't have good news.

'Dad, what is it?' she insisted.

'I'm so sorry, love,' he said, grimacing. 'Jayne had a work emergency after she dropped you home yesterday evening; she's been there all night.'

'Oh no,' said Claire, clearly disappointed.

'I hate to let you down, love, but we're going to have to **postpone** our theatre visit tomorrow. Some sort of **catastrophic** security **breach** has attacked the Via-Corp headquarters' systems, and I doubt she'll be able to get away this weekend. It's pretty serious stuff, I think,' he finished.

'Oh, that's a real shame, Dad. Could we go next weekend instead?' asked Claire hopefully.

'Maybe. I hope so, love. I'm sure Jayne will rebook the tickets as soon as she can,' he added.

'What's up?' asked Dee, clattering down the stairs into the lounge. She had changed out of her dressing gown into jeans and a shirt. Claire didn't miss the quick **application** of make-up; she suspected Dee would **reunite** with Vince in a heartbeat, given half a chance.

Poor Mum, she thought.

'What is it?' Dee asked again, staring at Vince.

'Er ... Jayne's needed at work this weekend, so we need to **reschedule** tomorrow,' said Vince, looking down as the spoke.

'Really? After her ordeal yesterday, you're letting Claire down?' said Dee, wagging her finger at him.

'Mum, it's fine,' said Claire, realising her mum's attempt at **capitalising** on the opportunity to **berate** Jayne. 'I'm going out with Ben today, anyway, and we're bound to be back late. It might be a good thing it's postponed. I'm a bit tired; it'll give me a chance to catch up,' said Claire, placating her mother.

'I'm sorry, Claire,' said Vince again.

'It's fine, Dad. Will you just ask Jayne to rebook as soon as she can?' said Claire, giving him a goodbye hug.

'Is Becs up yet?' he asked.

'She's in the shower,' replied Dee.

'Oh, OK,' said Vince. 'I'm really sorry, Dee,' he continued, nodding towards her. 'See you, Pete,' he added, reaching over to his sofa-**splayed** son and lifting one of the earpieces from the side of his head. 'See you, son,' he said again, letting go of it with a playful **twang**.

'See ya, Dad,' Pete replied, not taking his eyes off the screen.

'Would you ask Becs to give me a call later today, please?' Vince asked.

Dee didn't speak.

1 Which word in line 1 tells us that Dee would not give up until Claire did as asked?

A. 'now'

B. 'hissed'

C. 'low'

D. 'insistent'

2 What was Claire's first thought when her mother knocked on her door?

A. She thought her mother was angry.

B. She thought her sister was sick.

C. She thought her brother was missing.

D. She thought her father was visiting.

3 What is meant when it says Claire's 'earlier niggle' returned 'with a vengeance' (line 9)?

A. Her previous bad feeling came back strongly.

B. A lost pet came back to her.

C. She missed her father.

D. Her mother reminded her of something.

4 What was the bad news that Claire's father had?

A. They had to sell their house.

B. They had to delay their visit to the theatre.

C. They had to give away her things.

D. Her sister was ill again.

5 Choose a single word to substitute 'let you down' (line 18)?

A. drop

B. give

C. betray

D. disappoint

6 What happened at Jayne's company, according to Vince?

A. There was an explosion.

B. There was a security breach.

C. There was a loss of jobs.

D. There was a reduction in company spending.

7 What could Claire sense about the feelings her mother had for her father?

A. Her mother hated her father.

B. Her mother thought her father was funny.

C. Her mother wanted money from her father.

D. Her mother still had feelings for her father.

8 Why are the words 'Poor Mum' italicised (line 26)?

A. It shows what Claire wanted to say.

B. It shows Claire's thoughts.

C. It shows Claire's writing.

D. It shows what Claire planned to do.

9 Why is a semicolon used when Claire said, 'I'm a bit tired; it'll give me a chance to catch up' (line 33)?

A. to add an opinion

B. to add a thought

C. to add another relevant clause of equal importance

D. to add an explanation for current events

10 How could we describe Pete's farewell to his father?

A. Pete was preoccupied.

B. Pete was rude.

C. Pete was resentful.

D. Pete was overbearing.

SECTION 2 – LINKED WORDS

Select the word from the options that fits best with the words in both sets of brackets.

11 (convince, persuade) (rationale, logic)

A. manipulate	B. reason	C. influence	D. analytics	E. sell

12 (kitchen, dishes) (subside, drain)

A. cooker	B. soap	C. decrease	D. sink	E. brush

13 (penalty, monetary) (good, satisfactory)

A. price	B. fine	C. punishment	D. ideal	E. pass

14 (room, sitting) (slack, idle)

A. lounge	B. living	C. sofa	D. ease	E. relax

15 (face, skin) (disrespect, insolence)

A. eye	B. chin	C. cheek	D. challenge	E. upstart

SECTION 3 – VOCABULARY IN CONTEXT

Select the most appropriate option that matches the meaning of the word underlined in the sentence.

16 Vince walked past the sofa, heading for the front door.

A. Vince was thinking hard about something.

B. Vince was running with his head down.

C. Vince was walking in the direction of the door.

D. Vince hit his head while on the way to the door.

17 Vince straightened up, Claire's school bag in his hand.

A. Vince stood up straight.

B. Vince stopped making jokes.

C. Vince took some measurements.

D. Vince adjusted his surroundings to appear neater.

18 Speechless, her mind racing, her bag dangling from her hand, Claire stuttered.

A. Claire could not stop stuttering.

B. Claire was afraid of giving speeches.

C. Claire was going to give fewer speeches in the future.

D. Claire was so surprised that she didn't know what to say.

19 'It was outside my flat this morning with a note on the top of it.'

A. He had a flat tyre.

B. He lived in an apartment.

C. He spoke in a flat voice.

D. He had a letter box with a flat top.

20 'I didn't see her again last night, after dropping Becs here.'

A. He brought Rebecca there and left her.

B. He was carrying Rebecca but dropped her by accident.

C. He felt very tired after driving Rebecca there.

D. He tried to get Rebecca to go with him.

SECTION 4 – SPELLING ERRORS

Select the word in each group that has not been spelled correctly.

21	A. opulent	B. oppurtunity	C. opposition	D. opposable	E. opposite
22	A. application	B. apprehention	C. appalling	D. applicable	E. appetising
23	A. capitulating	B. capital	C. capricous	D. capitalising	E. capitol
24	A. playable	B. placeable	C. implacable	D. plient	E. placating
25	A. reunite	B. reinvent	C. reinforce	D. rectify	E. reimberse

SECTION 5 – COMPOUND WORDS

Underline a word from each set of brackets to make a new compound word.

26	(shower, bath, tub)	(room, hall, corridor)
27	(all, not, any)	(item, day, thing)
28	(some, partial, every)	(why, which, how)
29	(week, month, year)	(finish, end, climax)
30	(ear, nose, throat)	(piece, bit, thing)

WORKSHEET 21

SECTION 1 – COMPOUND WORDS

Select the option that forms a compound word once the blank is filled in.

1 She nearly forgot her _______ bag at the cafe.

A. purse	B. make	C. clasp	D. hand

2 I've outlined the _______ work needed to build the cottage.

A. home	B. frame	C. school	D. house

3 I'm at the _______ course watching the horses.

A. race	B. track	C. full	D. equestrian

4 You can _______ power him if you really want to.

A. current	B. under	C. over	D. electric

5 Stop giving me the run _______ and tell me the truth.

A. about	B. up	C. through	D. around

SECTION 2 – WORD DEFINITIONS

Choose the best definition for the given words.

6 admonish

A. reward
B. reverse
C. revere
D. reprimand

7 light-heartedly

A. done in a fun, casual way
B. done in a way to cause excitement
C. done in a serious manner
D. done in a half-hearted way

8 regally

A. done expensively
B. done majestically
C. done ceremoniously
D. done pompously

9 lilt

A. a singing voice

B. the intonation of someone's voice

C. the emotion in someone's voice

D. relating to lilies

10 trill

A. to make a warbling sound, like a bird

B. to make a perfect imitation of a songbird

C. to make a sound like the ringing of bells

D. to make a shrill, screeching sound

SECTION 3 – WORD DEFINITIONS

Select the definition that best matches the word.

A. a practical joke

B. to tell a lie

C. to disagree with another's actions

D. the rejection of an assignment

E. a device used to aid walking

F. information that has not yet been proved to be true

G. imitate something

H. an obstacle to make a test difficult

I. an alternative route

J. the latest news reports broadcast on live television

11	mock	________
12	disapprove	________
13	fib	________
14	detour	________
15	rumour	________

SECTION 4 – ANTONYM PAIRS

Which of the following pairs are NOT antonyms?

16
A. alert, wary
B. late, early
C. certain, unknown
D. likely, unpredictable
E. perceive, overlook

17
A. try, forfeit
B. query, answer
C. gullible, naive
D. conclusion, genesis
E. pinnacle, depths

18
A. withhold, divulge
B. investigate, ignore
C. ruin, improve
D. forgive, avenge
E. persist, endure

19
A. partake, resist
B. precipitation, drought
C. fancy, desire
D. reign, serve
E. rival, ally

20
A. triumphant, ineffective
B. bustling, deserted
C. foreboding, calm
D. solitude, companionship
E. abundant, bountiful

REVISION TESTS

These extra practice questions are mixed and ideal for use as timed tests.

REVISION TEST 1

SECTION 1 – COMPREHENSION

Read the passage and answer the questions that follow.

an extract from The Cadwaladr Quests – Tangled Time – Chapter 5. **Worse than Cross-Country**

After a while of constant climbing, Claire's finger touched a lip of rock. A ledge protruded outwards, and she hooked both hands over the top. She felt the ground with the flats of her hands. *Grass?* she thought. *Grass!*

'Jack, wait. Stay there, boy,' she ordered.

Mustering every muscle, she gave one final, mighty haul, let out a loud grunt and hoisted herself over the jutting ledge, rolling onto her side and flat onto her back in the grass.

'Yes!' she shouted. 'I did it!'

Claire gasped, every cell in her body screaming for oxygen. She stretched out starfish-shaped and started laughing, looking up at the clouds. She'd really made it.

Jack followed, **unceremoniously** leaping over the ledge easily and **plastering** her **filthy** face with **soggy** kisses.

'Thanks, Jack,' she laughed, pushing him away.

Completely drained and exhausted, she didn't want to move. The clouds floated above, rolling back and forth in **soporific** waves. She could have dozed off right there in the dirt, but she forced herself to roll over and edge her way back to the ledge, peering over the side.

'Wow, did I climb up that?' Claire marvelled at herself.

From here she could witness the **sheer** drop she'd climbed. Crawling closer to the edge, she realised in awe that its **rim** formed the **circumference** of a huge circle, its massive **diameter** stretching further than the eye could **discern**. A **crater**, like a **dormant** volcano, full of thick, overgrown bushes and trees. Up on the rim, in stark contrast, the tiny patch of grass she lay on quickly disappeared into a **sparse wilderness**. Huge piles of **rubble**, rocks and soil streaked a mixture of red and orange, and there were several reddish-green-tinged lakes. A faint **metallic** smell wafted in the air.

Dizzied by the **magnitude**, like a baby crawling in **reverse**, she backed away from the edge. Then suddenly Jack's loud barks caught her attention. She was still on all fours when she turned to see Gwilym striding towards her, Jack at his heels. Shocked, and now clear of the edge, she jumped to her feet.

'How come you left me?' Claire shouted. 'What happened to you and the other **bloke** I was supposed to be following? Some **lad** dragged me down the hill; he could have killed me!' she yelled even louder, pointing an **accusing** finger. 'Who was that boy, anyway?'

'But he didn't kill you, did he?' replied Gwilym calmly. 'That boy is a Mal-Instinctive; he was on one of the motorbikes. How did you escape him?'

Still angry, Claire thought about the **vulgar** excuse with which she'd **outwitted** the boy, but embarrassed, she **desisted** from divulging the full details to Gwilym.

'I threw Jack's lead at him,' she answered **flatly**.

Only as she spoke did the enormity of what she'd done hit her. 'It hit him on his forehead,' she mumbled, looking at Gwilym's **impassive** face watching hers.

'I didn't think I'd get away from him,' she cried, covering her face with her hands in horror at the memory of it.

1 What did Claire do when she felt ground above her?

A. She lifted herself up to the top.

B. She waited where she was.

C. She went back down.

D. She tried to climb around.

2 Why is the word 'grass' italicised on line 2?

A. for emphasis

B. to show Claire's thoughts

C. to highlight that Claire is shouting

D. to highlight Claire's anxiety

3 Why does 'grass' change from 'Grass?' to 'Grass!'?

A. to show uncertainty and then realisation

B. to show wonder and awe

C. to show puzzlement and fear

D. to show disdain and confusion

4 What is Claire's stretched-out form likened to?

A. a catfish

B. a shellfish

C. a starfish

D. a jellyfish

5 Which word tells us the clouds have a dreamy, sleep-inducing quality?

A. 'soggy'

B. 'soporific'

C. 'discern'

D. 'dormant'

6 What did the crater remind Claire of?

A. a dormant volcano

B. a sleeping giant

C. a big hole

D. a muddy puddle

7 What got Claire's attention?

A. Jack scratching

B. Jack barking

C. birds chirping

D. wolves howling

8 Why was Claire angry with Gwilym?

A. Gwilym had attacked her.

B. Gwilym had scared her.

C. Gwilym had chased her.

D. Gwilym had left her.

9 Which word in lines 31 to 35 tells us that Claire used her intelligence to get away from the boy?

A. 'vulgar'

B. 'outwitted'

C. 'desisted'

D. 'flatly'

10 Why did Claire cover her face when remembering her experience?

A. She was very happy.

B. She was trying not to laugh.

C. She was overwhelmed.

D. She was angry.

SECTION 2 – SYNONYMS

Select the word from the options that is closest in meaning to the word in **bold**.

11 'bellowing'

A. barking	B. ululating	C. roaring	D. clamouring	E. snarling

12 'pitch'

A. tone	B. perfect	C. blue	D. dark	E. treble

13 'erase'

A. demolish	B. bowdlerise	C. overtake	D. obliterate	E. exterminate

14 'incoherent'

A. scattered	B. not sticky	C. lucid	D. silly	E. unclear

15 'protruding'

A. discourteous	B. looming	C. sticking out	D. inconspicuous	E. distended

SECTION 3 – COMPOUND WORDS

Underline a word from each set of brackets to make a new compound word.

16	(hand, finger, wrist)	(particle, some, few)
17	(occupation, trade, business)	(child, boy, man)
18	(swan, goose, hen)	(bumps, bangs, thuds)
19	(elbow, shoulder, arm)	(seat, chair, sofa)
20	(apprentice, trainee, learner)	(yacht, boat, ship)

SECTION 4 – LINKED WORDS

Select the word from the options that fits best with the words in both sets of brackets.

21 (torso, breast) (trunk, box)

A. thorax	B. ottoman	C. sternum	D. crate	E. chest

22 (estimate, assess) (scale, meter)

A. judge	B. gauge	C. dial	D. evaluate	E. display

23 (catwalk, model) (create, construct)

A. fashion	B. invent	C. watch	D. wardrobe	E. building

24 (memorandum, record) (small, tiny)

A. microscopic	B. moment	C. meticulous	D. minute	E. summary

25 (frightened, terrified) (ossified, fossilised)

A. petrified	B. horrified	C. mortified	D. outmoded	E. scared

SECTION 5 – ODD WORD OUT

Select the odd word out in each set of words.

26	A. same	B. different	C. similar	D. alike	E. near
27	A. absurd	B. ludicrous	C. serious	D. risible	E. farcical
28	A. observation	B. scrutiny	C. surveillance	D. glance	E. inspection
29	A. dormant	B. wriggle	C. fidget	D. squirm	E. twitch
30	A. reflective	B. effective	C. pensive	D. meditative	E. contemplative

REVISION TEST 2

SECTION 1 – JUMBLED PARAGRAPHS

Choose the most logical order of sentences to construct a meaningful paragraph.

1
a) His tap turned the screen transparent, revealing the female driver.
b) Then he reclined into the decadent opulence of plush cream leather.
c) He tapped the opaque glass with his manicured fingernail.
d) He nodded to her and tapped the screen again to return it to privacy mode.

A. dbca	B. cadb	C. cbda	D. abdc

2
a) He inspected the rising amber bubbles.
b) He lifted the glass of champagne up towards the light.
c) The digital reader displayed the beverage's exact temperature.
d) He popped his minute thermometer into the champagne flute.

A. dbac	B. cabd	C. badc	D. acdb

3
a) His gesture caused a screen to glide down.
b) The screen halted at eye level.
c) He gesticulated with a dismissive wave.
d) He looked up at the roof.

A. dcab	B. bcad	C. acbd	D. acbd

4
a) She was too busy strapping herself into the front of Jayne's smart four-wheel drive.
b) Claire didn't see the chauffeur-driven black Bentley glide past them.
c) She narrowly missed the handsome, stylishly attired man in the back.
d) As her seat belt connected, she glanced outside.

A. dbca	B. badc	C. acdb	D. cadb

5
a) Why had the glass not succumbed to its targeted blows?
b) Fascinated, he studied the cutter between his fingers.
c) He held an oblong metal box in the other.
d) He rolled a matchstick-sized object in one hand.

A. cbad	B. dcba	C. cdab	D. dabc

SECTION 2 – CLOZE

Choose the most suitable word to fill in the gaps from the corresponding set of brackets.

With obvious barbaric **6** ______ *(aspiration, intent, hope, yearning)*, Drane roared and smashed the lamp down **7** ______ *(after, towards, sharply, inside)* his thigh. He hadn't noticed an **8** ______ *(unbiddable, obedient, unruly, obstreperous)* Jack drop down and sit beside Claire's feet just before the **9** ______ *(imaginary, makeshift, assumed, foolish)* battering ram bludgeoned into his flesh. When the **10** ______ *(godlike, invincible, impregnable, almighty)* impact struck, his legs collapsed underneath him.

SECTION 3 – MISSING LETTERS

Find the letters that have been removed from the word in CAPITALS. Once these letters are placed back in the word, the sentence will make sense.

11 She thought it might be the finest SWICH she had ever tasted.

A. in	B. at	C. the	D. and

12 She ALED herself a smile.

A. row	B. now	C. low	D. bow

13 One of her CLASSS holidayed in Wales most summers.

A. tram	B. mate	C. rate	D. tale

14 Claire REED a mite and rested her head against the window.

A. pax	B. max	C. tax	D. lax

15 She fumbled around in her bag PREING to fish something out.

A. tend	B. bent	C. sand	D. long

SECTION 4 – ADJECTIVES

Select the noun from the options that most closely relates to the adjective in **bold**.

16 masterful

A. dress	B. feet	C. stroll	D. stride	E. book

17 eloquent

A. dance	B. voice	C. song	D. shout	E. yell

18 fiery

A. hand	B. box	C. fan	D. sparks	E. laptop

19 capacious

A. wire	B. letter	C. hall	D. pillow	E. rug

20 persuasive

A. food	B. pen	C. pong	D. perfume	E. character

REVISION TEST 3

SECTION 1 – COMPREHENSION

Read the passage and answer the questions that follow.

an extract from The Cadwaladr Quests – Tangled Time – Chapter 1. **A Normal Day**

'Oh no, not you!' Claire stiffened, staring at the carpet.

'Wallace! No! No! No!' She thudded down onto **bare** knees. 'Wallace, what is it? What have I done to you?' she cried as the unfortunate scene **unfurled**.

She **shuffled** along on all fours, creeping closer, afraid of what lay on the floor. **Dithering** and uncertain, she **gingerly** lifted him to avoid more damage. As she realised it was worse than she'd thought, she almost dropped him. **Cradling** him, she tried and tried, but it was too late.

Her old friend was beyond repair.

As Claire gazed down at his broken body, her **earnest** face wore a mixture of love and **sorrow**. Tears glazed her eyes as **fond** childhood memories unfolded before her. Was this repairable? How could she fix this accident? She held him in her hand.

'I wonder if I could glue you,' she said, holding Gromit in the other hand. 'I'm such a clumsy **klutz**!'

A regretful smile separated the three friends. She tried to push him back together, but on closer **inspection**, she feared poor Wallace may well have been silenced forever.

Claire Cadwallader lived in Chorlton, Manchester, England. She enjoyed simple things, like her now-broken Wallace and Gromit alarm clock.

She **considered** books to be friends, living in her bedroom on dusty shelves. Not a massive fan of pop stars and fashion, she found even school **appealed**.

'I will try to mend you. Don't you worry, Wallace,' Claire said, forcing a cheery tone.

As if handling the Crown Jewels, she gathered up the broken pieces. Her dad had gifted the talking clock to her brother, Peter, on his fourth birthday. It belonged to her now, and she **cherished** it like a family **heirloom**.

Then, bang on time, as if an alarm had sounded, the shrieking **commenced**. Once Dee surfaced, so did the **commotion**. They lived in a shouty house.

'Here we go again.' Claire rolled her eyes and snatched at a pile of creased clothes.

'Peter, you're getting the wet flannel treatment! Come on now! Right this minute, I mean it! I'm not kidding this morning!'

On weekdays, **chaos** ruled. 'The wet flannel treatment' was the threat Dee, Claire's mum, gave Pete, Claire's older brother, every single schoolday yet never carried out.

'If you don't get up right now, I'm going to wet this flannel with freezing water, and it will head straight for you,' Dee **threatened** again.

'Yeah, right, Mum, course you are,' grumbled Claire, **barging** past Rebecca, her sister.

With a swift move to the right, a couple of smart steps to the left, she ducked through the bathroom door and locked it. 'First in this morning, ha!' she **gloated** out loud.

'Hurry up, Choccy **Eclair**,' Pete **whinged**, hammering on the door.

Most of her family called her 'Eclair'. She pretended it didn't bother her, but it did. She **tended** to be weak around chocolate.

To **irritate** her brother, Claire took ages cleaning her teeth. Struggling to see her blurred reflection through the **streaks** of splattered toothpaste, she **grimaced** and pulled funny faces at the **grimy** mirror. She sucked in her chubby cheeks for the mirror, posing. She lowered her eyelids and **pouted**, flicking her wavy hair with a **flamboyant flourish**. Claire would never be a model. Still, acting like one was fun. Crossing her eyes and poking out her tongue, she thought of her dad and Jayne coming to visit at the weekend.

Her parents had recently separated. She missed her dad every day but hid her guilty relief.

They had argued badly towards the end, and home had improved without it. Yet things weren't so bad. Claire liked her dad's new girlfriend, Jayne, although her mum and sister **despised** her. Dee insisted that Jayne had been the reason her dad had left, yet Jayne's kindness hadn't **wavered** since she had met her, so Claire judged as she found.

'Will you hurry up?' Pete yelled, banging on the door again.

'I'm coming now,' she fibbed, thinking of the weekend.

Rebecca no longer spoke to her dad, and Pete didn't care either way, so Jayne had **reserved theatre** tickets in town, just for the three of them. Claire hadn't seen a live performance before, and she was so excited she'd spent the week **reverting** to toddler behaviour, counting the sleeps.

They'd booked an **expensive** restaurant too; she might even be reduced to scrounging clothes from Rebecca. Claire's wardrobe consisted of jeans, hoodies and trainers.

'Can't work out what Princess Jayne sees in your dad,' her mum would **snipe**. 'She's too **grand** for him. She's **snared** him, and why? What's he got to offer her? Doesn't add up.'

Claire put the **former** down to her dad's **charming** good looks, and the **latter** – her mum's **peevishness** – to jealousy. And why shouldn't her mum be jealous? She'd lost her husband to a **sophisticated** beauty with a high-powered job, no nuisance kids and a gorgeous home. No wonder Dee **loathed** her.

Claire loved her mum, though she didn't always like her. Same with her sister. Both were so different from her. Peas in a pod. Hair, make-up, fashion. Often, in Claire's **humble** opinion, not the most tasteful. Recently her mum reminded her of an over-iced cupcake.

Her brother's **persistent** hammering and football-style **chants** of 'Come on, Eclair! Come on, Eclair!' **jolted** Claire back to her toothbrush. Slimy, foamed toothpaste dribbled down her hand and onto the sleeve of her navy school jumper, leaving a white trail in its **wake**.

'Doh!' she muttered, rubbing at the stain, smearing it into a smudgy blob.

1 What did Claire intend to do with her broken clock?

A. She intended to throw it away.

B. She intended to fix it.

C. She intended to give it away.

D. She intended to recycle it.

2 What kind of house does Claire live in?

A. a noisy house

B. a quiet house

C. a tidy house

D. a large house

3 What did Claire's mother threaten to do to Pete?

A. She threatened to take away Pete's phone.

B. She threatened to take Pete's pocket money.

C. She threatened to throw a wet facecloth at Pete.

D. She threatened to not give Pete any lunch.

4 Which of the following was Claire unable to resist?

A. chips

B. burgers

C. chocolate

D. liquorice

5 What did Claire do to irritate Pete?

A. She used all the hot water.

B. She took a long time brushing her teeth.

C. She used his favourite shampoo.

D. She used all the toothpaste.

6 What did Claire pretend to be while in the bathroom?

A. She pretended to be a model.

B. She pretended to be her mother.

C. She pretended to be her sister.

D. She pretended to be a fish.

7 Why was Claire not living with both her parents?

A. Her father was dead.

B. Her father worked abroad.

C. Her parents had separated.

D. Her mother travelled a lot.

8 Which word between lines 11 and 15 means the opposite of 'careful'?

A. 'unfurled'

B. 'dithering'

C. 'fond'

D. 'clumsy'

9 Find a synonym for 'fix' between lines 16 and 21.

A. 'cherished'

B. 'commotion'

C. 'mend'

D. 'snatched'

10 What does the idiom 'peas in a pod' mean (line 61)?

A. twins

B. two people who have very similar interests, likes and dislikes

C. two peas still in their pod

D. a double bean pod

SECTION 2 – WORD DEFINITIONS

Select the definition that best suits the word in **bold**.

11 'poised'

A. showing a lack of physical grace

B. agitated and confused

C. appearing troubled or nervous

D. composed and self-assured

E. highly strung

12 'frantic'

A. the absence of strong emotions

B. distraught with fear or anxiety

C. not easily disturbed or angered

D. to give strength or energy to

E. calm, dignified, unhurried

13 'incoherent'

A. expressed in a confusing manner

B. forming a unified whole

C. lack of support for an idea

D. written language expressed clearly and concisely

E. dying without leaving any money

14 'queasy'

A. unconcerned and unruffled

B. being comfortable and feeling healthy

C. in good physical or mental condition

D. physical ease and relaxation

E. feeling slightly sick, nauseous

15 'gloomy'

A. vivid and colourful

B. shining brightly

C. dark or poorly lit

D. smouldering and flickering

E. misty and wet

SECTION 3 – ANAGRAMS

Rearrange the letters of the word on the left to make a suitable word for the sentence on the right.

16	CINE	He muttered, ' ☐☐☐☐ one, our kid.'
17	PRUDES	Pete ☐☐☐☐☐☐ his lips.
18	RING	With a fleeting ☐☐☐☐, he joined her.
19	BRIDES	Her mum was surrounded by cosmetic ☐☐☐☐☐☐ .
20	BLEARY	She was ☐☐☐☐☐☐ able to clear a path through the discarded shoes.

SECTION 4 – LINKED WORDS

Select the word from the options that fits best with the words in both sets of brackets.

21 (material, substance) (subject, topic)

A. issue	B. stuff	C. matter	D. constituent	E. theme

22 (touched, prodded) (cloth, textile)

A. material	B. felt	C. poked	D. jabbed	E. fondled

23 (retain, withhold) (stronghold, fortress)

A. possess	B. turret	C. conceal	D. maintain	E. keep

24 (rebelling, agitating) (horrible, disgusting)

A. fighting	B. revolting	C. appalling	D. sickening	E. nauseating

25 (bounce, ricochet) (look, peek)

A. glance	B. recoil	C. spring	D. spy	E. peer

SECTION 5 – SPELLING ERRORS

Select the word in each group that has not been spelled correctly.

26	A. literaly	B. exactly	C. precisely	D. really	E. indirectly
27	A. untidiness	B. shambles	C. chaos	D. dissaray	E. disorder
28	A. anarchy	B. authority	C. regime	D. administration	E. goverment
29	A. different	B. micsellanious	C. assorted	D. various	E. identical
30	A. massive	B. supreme	C. allmighty	D. enormous	E. powerful

REVISION TEST 4

SECTION 1 – HOMOPHONES

From the available choices, select the most appropriate option.

1 I ________ my family with me ________ now.

A. wont, want	B. want, write	C. wont, right	D. want, right

2 She held his gaze, not flinching ________ until he lowered his ________.

A. ones, eyes	B. ones, ice	C. once, eyes	D. once, ice

3 Claire ________ as he seemed to fight a ________ choke.

A. posed, sleight	B. paused, slight	C. paused, sleight	D. posed, slight

4 She tried in ________ to ________ his mind.

A. vain, read	B. vane, reed	C. vane, read	D. vain, reed

5 She couldn't ________ any of ________ thoughts.

A. hear, there	B. here, there	C. hear, their	D. here, their

SECTION 2 – ANTONYMS

Choose the word that is most opposite to the word on the left.

6	bleary	A. blurry	B. clear	C. stormy	D. funny
7	haze	A. befuddlement	B. obscurity	C. spray	D. lucidity
8	hectic	A. fast	B. orderly	C. feverish	D. restless
9	punctual	A. tardy	B. dependable	C. timely	D. prompt
10	astonished	A. drunk	B. amazed	C. underwhelmed	D. astounded

SECTION 3 – SPELLING ERRORS

Select the word in each group that has not been spelled correctly.

11	A. shriveled	B. stale	C. translucent	D. totter	E. edible
12	A. snigger	B. trifle	C. inccesant	D. ceaseless	E. constant
13	A. irregular	B. guess	C. estimation	D. absalute	E. total
14	A. indesicive	B. ponder	C. bitter	D. flutter	E. fossil
15	A. angry	B. fierce	C. extraordinary	D. wonderful	E. magnifisent

SECTION 4 – ODD WORD OUT

Select the odd word out in each set of words.

16	A. betrayal	B. duplicity	C. loyalty	D. treachery
17	A. mismanage	B. govern	C. regulate	D. oversee
18	A. greedy	B. rapacious	C. grasping	D. generous
19	A. gallant	B. craven	C. valiant	D. intrepid
20	A. sincere	B. profound	C. shallow	D. weighty

REVISION TEST 5

SECTION 1 – COMPREHENSION

Read the passage and answer the questions that follow.

an extract from The Cadwaladr Quests – Tangled Time – Chapter 21. **Another Unexpected Change of Plan**

'It's quite a drive today, son. The **organiser** has changed it at the last minute,' he replied. 'It's in North Wales now.'

North Wales! thought Claire, jolted into high alert.

'Wow, North Wales,' she remarked, trying to sound breezy. 'Where in North Wales, Mr Brady?'

'Bangor,' he replied.

Claire gulped, briefly catching his eye in his rear-view mirror. She quickly looked away.

'You OK, Claire?' asked Ben. 'You seem different. Is something bothering you?' he persisted.

'Nah. I'm cool. Just tired after yesterday,' she said, looking out of the window again. 'My mum flipped, and I couldn't get to sleep.'

She was desperate to share her story with him, but instead, she just stared at the same countryside she had passed through on the train to Bangor yesterday.

'Dad, any chance you could turn Radio Bore off and put Radio One on, please?' Ben asked, laughing.

'Sure, son,' replied Mr Brady just as the phone rang through the car's speakers, interrupting the music. The name 'William C' flashed up onto the Tesla's screen.

'You gonna kill that call, Dad?' moaned Ben as the ringing persisted, blocking out the music.

'It's work,' replied his dad after a few seconds. 'I fancy a coffee, so I'll stop at the services, give the car a charge and call them back then.'

'It's Saturday, Dad; ignore it,' said Ben, laughing.

'That's why I *won't* ignore it, Ben,' replied his dad. 'They wouldn't call me if it wasn't important.'

*

'Don't even ask,' said Mr Brady to Ben and Claire, who stood drooling over a glass cabinet containing American-style doughnuts. He clutched a large coffee in one hand, and his phone in the other. 'Come on, you two,' he said, nodding towards the exit of the services' bustling main **thoroughfare**.

'Change of plan,' said Mr Brady, unplugging the Tesla. 'Jump in and I'll fill you in,' he finished.

Claire's stomach clenched. She climbed into the back of the car, trembling so much she could barely fasten her seat belt.

Mr Brady turned to face them in the back. 'I'm really sorry, guys, but the competition is off.'

'Oh no! Why?' asked a disappointed Ben.

Claire dreaded what Mr Brady might say next.

'I'm sorry, but I have to go into work, son,' he began. 'There's been a huge security breach overnight, and they're calling everyone in. It's **all hands on deck**,' he finished.

Security breach, thought Claire. She had heard those words already today, from her dad. Hadn't that been why Jayne had gone into work too?

'All's not lost though,' Mr Brady continued. 'Our headquarters are in the Welsh mountains, so I don't have to go back to the Manchester office. I'll get you two a work phone for the day, and you can go **sightseeing** in the village whilst I go in and help. If you're *really* lucky, you might see some low-flying fighter jets circling the **Mach Loop**, where the pilots train. It's all in the company's grounds, so you'll be safe,' he finished.

'Hey, that would be soooo cool, Dad,' said Ben, beaming at Claire.

'Yeah, great,' added Claire. 'Sounds fun,' she said, trying to sound enthusiastic. 'Where do you work, Mr Brady?' she asked, her voice hollow.

'I work for a company called Via-Corp,' he answered, glancing at her in the mirror.

'Oh,' she replied, her heart banging in her chest.

It was the same company Jayne worked for and the same reason she, too, had been called in. Claire swallowed hard, trying to steady her voice. 'Where are we heading now, then, Mr Brady? Where are the headquarters?'

'Oh, they're on the outskirts of a quaint little place, quite a famous place though – in Wales, that is,' he added. 'It's called Beddgelert.'

1 **What made Claire start to worry immediately?**

A. They were driving to a place from Claire's childhood.

B. They were driving to North Wales.

C. She thought her brother was missing.

D. She thought her father was visiting.

2 **Why did Ben ask his father to 'kill that call'?**

A. It was giving him a headache.

B. It was distracting him.

C. It was drowning out the music.

D. It was affecting his father's driving.

3 **Apart from the model of the car being mentioned, how can we tell it is electric?**

A. It is able to take a phone call.

B. It has low mileage.

C. It needs to be charged.

D. It is unable to tackle tough terrain.

4 **What did Mr Brady mean when he said, 'I'll fill you in' (line 24)?**

A. He would give them some food.

B. He would give them more information.

C. He would draw a picture of them.

D. He would let Claire drive the car.

5 **Find the word that tells us Claire was scared about the upcoming events.**

A. 'disappointed'

B. 'dreaded'

C. 'great'

D. 'enthusiastic'

6 **What is meant by 'all hands on deck' (line 31)?**

A. They were going on a boat trip.

B. They needed everyone to help.

C. They were going to clean a house.

D. They had to work on a ship.

7 **What did Mr Brady suggest Ben and Claire do?**

A. They should go sightseeing.

B. They should go skiing.

C. They should go hiking.

D. They should go home.

8 How did Ben show enthusiasm for his father's decision?

A. He turned up the music.

B. He danced.

C. He dragged out the word 'so'.

D. He thanked his father profusely.

9 Why did Claire become so worried?

A. Ben's father was tired.

B. Ben's father was angry.

C. Ben's father worked for the same company as Jayne.

D. Ben's father expressed interest in Mal-Instinctive ideals.

10 What is Claire experiencing whilst learning about the location of Via-Corp's headquarters?

A. a spiritual awakening

B. a rush of joy

C. an unwelcome sense of unease

D. an epiphany

SECTION 2 – COMPOUND WORDS

Underline a word from each set of brackets to make a new compound word.

11	(some, sparse, few)	(who, how, why)
12	(core, hub, heart)	(shattered, burst, broken)
13	(digit, finger, sliver)	(print, impress, stamp)
14	(sister, daughter, girl)	(playmate, friend, companion)
15	(under, beneath, below)	(divulged, announced, stated)

SECTION 3 – REPLACE THE WORD

In each of the following sentences, replace one word with a word from the word bank so that the sentence continues to make sense.

A	B	C	D	E
mercilessness	clever	error	discovered	changing

16	He had misjudged her; he wouldn't make that mistake twice.
17	What had the shrewd little knight Evans done to it?
18	He'd lost deals before but always found other ways to win.
19	He had plenty of resilience and ruthlessness.
20	Columns of rapid figures flickered, shifting from red to green.

SECTION 4 – ADJECTIVES

Select the noun from the options that most closely relates to the adjective in **bold**.

21 despicable

A. paper	B. laptop	C. act	D. theatre	E. costume

22 brittle

A. mattress	B. sky	C. eraser	D. bone	E. cloud

23 willowy

A. total	B. sum	C. number	D. integer	E. figure

24 imminent

A. capital	B. war	C. covering	D. destiny	E. distance

25 counting

A. water	B. dark	C. happiness	D. sheep	E. light

SECTION 5 – RHYMING

Find a word that rhymes with the word on the left to complete the sentence.

26	RATIONAL	He sang his N A _ _ O _ _ L anthem with all his heart.
27	LITTLE	The shield was B R _ _ T _ E.
28	PERSISTENT	He was I _ S _ S T _ _ T on meeting in person.
29	YANKED	The radio wave B L _ _ K _ D out the phone signal.
30	NUMERIC	Pharmacies stock a lot of G _ _ E _ I C medication.

REVISION TEST 6

SECTION 1 – ANAGRAMS
Rearrange the letters of the word on the left to make a suitable word for the sentence on the right.

1	BUSTLE	Claire was thrown by the ☐☐☐☐☐☐ change of appearance in Gladys.
2	TEND	There was a large ☐☐☐☐ in the car door.
3	LIFT	I knew the birds would ☐☐☐☐ around the garden.
4	FRAIL	You have an innate ☐☐☐☐☐ for publicity.
5	ALLOY	She was kind, ☐☐☐☐☐ and had profound integrity.

SECTION 2 – CHANGE ONE LETTER
Change just one letter in the word on the left to create a new word that matches the description given.

6	pope	deal with something difficult	________
7	dint	a small hollow in a surface	________
8	slave	take a small amount from something	________
9	bail	cry or shout noisily	________
10	glad	annoy or provoke into a reaction	________

SECTION 3 – CLOZE
Choose the word that best completes the sentence.

11 She laughed to herself as she __________ the doughnut out of the bread bin.

A. crushed	B. made	C. squeezed	D. hooked	E. spat

12 Claire ________ up the dirty plates.

A. helped	B. presented	C. scooped	D. pinged	E. carted

13 Rebecca was _______ asleep on the couch.

A. awful	B. very	C. complete	D. slight	E. fast

14 Claire _________ a kiss on her mum's cheek.

A. planted	B. sowed	C. dug	D. struck	E. whacked

15 He shook her so hard I saw ______. I just flipped.

A. pink	B. mauve	C. blue	D. green	E. red

SECTION 4 – ANTONYMS
Choose the word that is most opposite to the word on the left.

16	renegade	A. rebel	B. follower	C. squire	D. defender
17	nervous	A. worried	B. intense	C. ecstatic	D. relaxed
18	lenient	A. unwavering	B. loose	C. compassionate	D. nimble
19	copious	A. ample	B. infrequent	C. sparse	D. unusual
20	prompt	A. early	B. late	C. immediate	D. incremental

REVISION TEST 7 

SECTION 1 – COMPREHENSION

Read the passage and answer the questions that follow.

an extract from The Cadwaladr Quests – Tangled Time – Chapter 11. **Teamwork**

'Dewi, stop!' the Welsh voice boomed from outside the office.

That's Gwilym, thought Claire, panicking at his tone bellowing from the empty hall.

The pitch of Gwilym's voice terrified her. Unable to think, her brain seemed to **erase** all **rational** thoughts. Mrs Evans was still writhing on the office floor, and her sister was drooling, **incoherent** in the chair. Josh Drane laughed. Gwilym **hollered** again, even louder this time.

What should I do? she thought.

She felt as if time had stopped and the world was **unravelling**.

Slumping back against a protruding **lintel**, too dazed to feel the impact against her back, Claire started to cry. She wished she was anywhere but here. If only she could be at home. A **torrent** of tears flowed in loud, **inconsolable** sobs. No longer **coping**, she cried and cried.

What's that scratching noise? she thought, wiping her eyes. But she only looked up when a dull thump hit the office door.

Whack! It happened again, followed by an incessant scratching and persistent yapping.

'Jack?' she called. 'Jack!'

'*Ruff! Ruff!*' Jack barked louder.

Claire lunged at the door and yanked it open with such force that the handle hit the wall, making a **dent**.

A blur of legs and teeth snarled its way into the room. Jack went straight for Drane, obviously meaning business. He leaped, landing square in the boy's lap, and sank his sharp canines into the soft, fleshy part of his thigh. Drane howled. Jerking, he wheeled around from left to right, filling the cramped space, bouncing off the walls. His hands swooped and slapped in **involuntary thrashes**, yet he didn't manage to hit Jack even once.

'Gerroff! Gerroff me!' he screamed.

His long legs **lashed** up and down in ridiculous **spasmodic** scissor kicks. Veering sideways, he spun in comical circles, trying to shake Jack off while a line of blood trickled down his torn trousers. Drane's arms flapped and **flailed, emulating** a windmill, but Jack's jaw was locked to his leg like a **vice**.

Stumbling again, Drane snatched at a solid metal reading lamp perched on a desk in the corner. With a violent yank, the plug ripped out of the wall, whipping across the room towards Claire's face. Her head jerked backwards with a gross twist, **wrenching** her neck. She managed to avoid the plug's metal **prongs** as they careered **haphazardly** towards her, **shaving** her nose by a millimetre. Recovering her balance, she saw Drane lifting the heavy lamp, his arms extended high above his head. Letting out a vicious war cry, he hurled it down towards the terrier hanging from his thigh.

'Jack, off!' screamed Claire as she watched Josh Drane with horror.

1 Which word in the first five lines of the text tells us that Gwilym was shouting very loudly?

A. 'boomed'

B. 'panicking'

C. 'pitch'

D. 'incoherent'

2 What caused Claire to panic?

A. She couldn't find her dog.

B. She wanted to go home.

C. She was afraid for Dewi's safety.

D. She was frightened by the pitch of Gwilym's voice.

3 Which word in lines 5 to 10 tells us that Claire was unable to be comforted when crying?

A. 'unravelling'

B. 'torrent'

C. 'inconsolable'

D. 'coping'

4 '*Whack!*' (line 13) is an example of ...

A. exclamation

B. onomatopoeia

C. oxymoron

D. interjection

5 How did Claire react to Jack's barks?

A. She leaped into action and flung open the door.

B. She stayed on the floor, crying.

C. She approached the door with caution.

D. She screamed.

6 What does 'a blur of legs and teeth' (line 17) tell us about the way Jack was moving?

A. Jack had brought other dogs with him.

B. Jack was moving so fast that it was difficult to see him clearly.

C. Jack had lights and mirrors attached to his body.

D. Jack had attached springs to his legs and was jumping.

7 How was Drane's speech affected by Jack's attack?

A. His speech was slurred.

B. He stuttered.

C. His voice became squeaky.

D. He screamed.

8 What is Jack's grip likened to?

A. a crocodile

B. a shark

C. a vice

D. a hyena

9 Which of these words is the best antonym for 'haphazardly' (line 29)?

A. systematically

B. carelessly

C. garishly

D. randomly

10 How did Claire try to get Jack away from Drane?

A. She pulled at Jack's legs.

B. She pushed Drane away.

C. She gave Jack a command to stop.

D. She helped Jack by kicking Drane.

SECTION 2 – REPLACE THE WORD

In each of the following sentences, replace one word with a word from the word bank so that the sentence continues to make sense.

A	B	C	D	E
rummaged	faintly	evading	thrust	slid

11 The basement was dimly lit.

12 He plunged his surroundings into darkness.

13 His feet skidded through the basement passages.

14 He delved into the sodden pocket of his waistcoat.

15 All hope of eluding the Master was gone.

SECTION 3 – SHUFFLED SENTENCES

Rearrange the words to form a meaningful sentence and find the superfluous word.

16 anger of the burned throat in a his bitter bile stream

17 unfamiliar sedate rural and Claire enjoyed eating the views

18 emerging undulating on the other side she greasy saw hills

19 the it summer felt like first week of the holidays likewise

20 Claire the for peered through looking window for Gladys

SECTION 4 – SYNONYMS

Select the word from the options that is closest in meaning to the word in **bold** on the left.

21	**unfurl**	A. reveal	B. expand	C. explain	D. divulge
22	**cradle**	A. grasp	B. hold	C. nestle	D. bolster
23	**fond**	A. attentive	B. tender	C. solicitous	D. benign
24	**klutz**	A. ignoramus	B. clown	C. dupe	D. butterfingers
25	**bare**	A. bald	B. barren	C. basic	D. empty

SECTION 5 – HOMOPHONES

Choose the word that corresponds to the correct spelling for the given definition.

26	to look quickly or furtively	peak	peek
27	a banner	sine	sign
28	to make an untrue statement	lie	lye
29	moved in a specific direction	past	passed
30	a deceptive or pretend blow	faint	feint

REVISION TEST 8 

SECTION 1 – MISSING LETTERS

Find the letters that have been removed from the word in CAPITALS. Once these letters are placed back in the word, the sentence will make sense.

1 The lock was so CORED she struggled to turn the key.

A. din	B. dog	C. rod	D. rib

2 She jiggled it LATE with small movements back and forth.

A. lley	B. sttly	C. ntlly	D. rally

3 The DISCOED, stiff hinges creaked laboriously open.

A. lour	B. leer	C. late	D. tour

4 Claire was APED at the paltry size of the prison cell.

A. sede	B. apel	C. clap	D. pall

5 The grim bed REED smoothly, slotting flush and unseen into the wall.

A. trace	B. tract	C. reck	D. trunk

SECTION 2 – SPELLING ERRORS

Select the word in each group that has not been spelled correctly.

6	A. staring	B. steadfastly	C. occasional	D. collossal	E. canine
7	A. chiseled	B. sculpted	C. ruddy	D. shovels	E. tinged
8	A. divulged	B. indescribable	C. veins	D. intrecate	E. etchings
9	A. amounted	B. unforseen	C. entire	D. gleamed	E. muscular
10	A. canopied	B. gnarled	C. sinister	D. rhythmic	E. exilerating

SECTION 3 – CLOZE

Choose the correct words from the table to fill in the gaps in the text.

A	B	C	D	E	F	G	H	I	J
deposited	maturation	scurried	moist	unfolded	swollen	incubator	nook	fortuitously	foraging

Whilst Claire slept at home, more truth to the story **11** ____________ deep in the underground tunnels. Busy **12** ____________ for food in the damp black recess, beetles, bugs and insects **13** ____________ about their daily duties. A **14** ____________ cocoa-brown cockroach **15** ____________ her precious eggs in the peaceful **16** ____________ crevice she had **17** ____________ discovered in the **18** ____________ behind the man's knees. This unusual **19** ____________ had lain still long enough to present her with the ideal hatching place for her egg case, although she didn't realise her eggs would never quite reach their forty-something days required for **20** ____________ .

REVISION TEST 9

SECTION 1 – COMPREHENSION

Read the passage and answer the questions that follow.

an extract from The Cadwaladr Quests – Tangled Time – Chapter 7. **The Race for the Cutter**

Upstairs in the stuffy cinema, Rebecca Cadwallader was oblivious to her sister's timely arrival in the **basement** beneath her. In fact, Rebecca Cadwallader was becoming oblivious to anything.

'Sir, Rebecca's not well,' Josh Drane called to his teacher, interrupting the film. His **bogus** act of caring and **civil** behaviour deserved an award.

'What's the matter, Drane?' replied Mr Hollie, looking dubiously at his pupil.

'Dunno, sir. She's acting funny and she's hot. She says she's gonna faint. I don't think she's putting it on,' replied Drane slimily.

The powdered drug he'd **administered** to Rebecca's drink would keep her feeling unwell, though not so ill as to pressure the teacher to cancel the trip. Rebecca would **comply** with Drane and, better still, afterwards remember nothing.

'Rebecca, how are you? What's wrong?' whispered Mr Hollie, approaching her seat.

The other pupils **craned** their necks to look as whispers rapidly spread around the hushed cinema. Clearly, they needed little excuse to distract them from the educational film – they had no interest in following it.

'I feel funny, sir. A bit weird and boiling hot. I want to lie down.'

Drane watched the teacher study the telltale **sheen** of sweat on Rebecca's **wan** face as she **slurred** her words.

Mr Hollie sniffed, then sighed. 'This is all I need,' he said, tutting.

'Mmm, she's sober,' he muttered to himself. 'I can't detect any trace of **alcohol**.'

'Drane, stay here with Rebecca and Miss Malik. I'll be right back. I'm going to ask Mr Evans for help. She needs to lie down somewhere.'

'Course, sir,' replied Drane, his face portraying a picture of concern.

Mr Hollie turned with an irritated groan towards his assistant.

'Miss Malik, Rebecca Cadwallader isn't feeling well. Stay with her and **supervise** the class while I **confer** with Mr Evans, the museum's curator,' he demanded imperiously.

Not waiting for her answer, he hurried out.

Outside the cinema door, he almost rammed into the curator. 'Oh, good, Mr Evans,' he blurted.

'Is everything all right, Mr Hollie?' **queried** Mr Evans. 'The film has a while to run yet.'

'One of my pupils is unwell. Could she lie down somewhere? Hopefully, it won't be for long,' said the teacher. 'I'm sure there's no real **malady**, but it is rather hot and stuffy in there,' he added in a **pompous** manner.

'Oh dear, I am sorry. We have an office with a **reclining** chair. She can rest there with my wife, if that helps,' replied Mr Evans.

'Yes, please. Thank you, and sorry for the **inconvenience**,' replied the teacher.

Mr Evans spoke into a **clunky** walkie-talkie radio, requesting his wife be asked to come to the cinema urgently.

1 **Which word in the first five lines means the opposite of 'airy'?**

A. 'stuffy'

B. 'oblivious'

C. 'bogus'

D. 'civil'

2 Which word tells us that Josh was not sincere?

A. 'oblivious'

B. 'bogus'

C. 'powdered'

D. 'excuse'

3 What was the real cause of Rebecca not feeling well?

A. an energy drink

B. caffeine

C. a powdered drug

D. a food allergy

4 Find an informal way of saying 'unwell' within the text.

A. 'stuffy'

B. 'funny'

C. 'comply'

D. 'pressure'

5 What grammatical device is used to indicate an explanation will be given for the students being easily distracted?

A. question mark

B. semicolon

C. dash

D. hyphen

6 Why did Mr Hollie initially think Rebecca was intoxicated?

A. Rebecca was dancing on the tables and chairs.

B. Rebecca was singing loudly and out of tune.

C. Rebecca was stumbling around the room.

D. Rebecca was unable to articulate her speech coherently.

7 Find a word in the text that is the opposite of 'intoxicated'.

A. 'telltale'

B. 'sheen'

C. 'wan'

D. 'sober'

8 Which of these indicates that Mr Hollie has an aloof manner of speaking?

A. He uses too many pronouns.

B. He belittles his superiors.

C. He speaks in a pompous way.

D. He uses too many similes.

9 **What is a curator?**

A. someone who looks after museum or other collections

B. someone who collects stamps

C. someone who critiques art

D. someone who looks for cures for common illnesses

10 **What is the best way to describe Mr Evans's tone towards Mr Hollie?**

A. demeaning and insincere

B. concerned and apologetic

C. apathetic and vehement

D. belligerent and unaccommodating

SECTION 2 – LINKED WORDS

Select the word from the options that fits best with the words in both sets of brackets.

11 (bedroom, bed) (tomb, vault)

A. scratch	B. heavy	C. dignified	D. chamber	E. serious

12 (remote, volume) (silent, voiceless)

A. island	B. loud	C. mute	D. hit	E. bang

13 (circlet, band) (chime, resonate)

A. toll	B. ring	C. tinkle	D. peal	E. hoop

14 (remain, adhere) (wood, branch)

A. abide	B. stick	C. booth	D. tripod	E. trivet

15 (fright, scare) (clock, time)

A. mass	B. alarm	C. jar	D. bombshell	E. cascade

SECTION 3 – COMPOUND WORDS

Underline a word from each set of brackets to make a new compound word.

16	(foot, leg, finger)	(hand, ball, toe)
17	(mug, cup, saucer)	(wood, plank, board)
18	(dough, flour, sugar)	(screw, nut, bolt)
19	(mouth, ear, nose)	(shot, gun, bullet)
20	(bald, head, hair)	(drawer, chest, dresser)

SECTION 4 – ODD WORD OUT

Select the odd word out in each set of words.

21	A. attentive	B. distracted	C. alert	D. observant
22	A. explicit	B. definite	C. established	D. tentative
23	A. comfort	B. disconcert	C. reassure	D. soothe
24	A. affectionate	B. austere	C. unfeeling	D. cold
25	A. calm	B. tranquil	C. fraught	D. unruffled

SECTION 5 – ANAGRAMS

Rearrange the letters of the word on the left to make a suitable word for the sentence on the right.

26	LARGE	Claire shot her sister a death ☐☐☐☐☐ instead.
27	ETHER	All ☐☐☐☐☐ siblings had inherited their dad's curly hair.
28	DIPOLES	Ben was an only child but not a ☐☐☐☐☐☐☐ child.
29	OUTSOURCE	John Brady seemed too ☐☐☐☐☐☐☐☐☐ and discreet.
30	THICKEN	Hanging up in Claire's ☐☐☐☐☐☐☐ were her mum's hair straighteners.

REVISION TEST 10

SECTION 1 – ADJECTIVES

Select the noun from the options that most closely relates to the adjective in **bold**.

1 **automatic**

A. ashes	B. embers	C. coal	D. ignition	E. candle

2 **complex**

A. wallet	B. case	C. receptacle	D. container	E. bag

3 **sheepish**

A. gaze	B. look	C. stare	D. gape	E. ogle

4 **dishevelled**

A. furniture	B. air	C. outcome	D. clothes	E. carpets

5 **scuffed**

A. socks	B. hats	C. shoes	D. gloves	E. braces

SECTION 2 – SPELLING ERRORS

Select the word in each group that has not been spelled correctly.

6	A. moreover	B. loyal	C. integrity	D. luducrous	E. reliable
7	A. blossom	B. nonsensical	C. absurd	D. suceed	E. flourish
8	A. forecast	B. predict	C. aptitude	D. competence	E. capibility
9	A. opportunity	B. prospect	C. occassion	D. melancholy	E. constituent
10	A. initiate	B. instegate	C. commence	D. instruct	E. facilitate

SECTION 3 – RHYMING

Find a word that rhymes with the word on the left to complete the sentence.

11	TWIRLED	A smell of fresh lilies [S][W][ ][ ][L][ ][D] upwards.
12	EFFECTIVELY	The woman wrapped her arm [P][R][ ][ ][E][C][ ][I][ ][E][L][Y] around me.
13	DILAPIDATED	The policeman [I][N][ ][ ][S][ ][ ][G][ ][T][ ][D] the attempted theft.
14	POUNCING	Hollie was flapping and [F][L][O][ ][ ][ ][I][ ][G] about.
15	CONFETTI	His spindly legs buckled like [S][ ][A][G][ ][ ][ ][ ][T][ ].

SECTION 4 – REPLACE THE WORD

In each of the following sentences, replace one word with a word from the word bank so that the sentence continues to make sense.

A	B	C	D	E
questionably	justified	balanced	scribbled	carelessly

16	Her food warranted a government health warning.
17	She would leave a scrawled note.
18	Her mum perched on the chair.
19	His trainers skated blithely across the room.
20	She rattled a suspiciously light box.

REVISION TEST 11

SECTION 1 – COMPREHENSION

Read the passage and answer the questions that follow.

an extract from The Cadwaladr Quests – Tangled Time – Chapter 15. **Sticking to the Story**

'Yeah, I'm fine, Dad. I'm really, really sorry for not going to school. You're not too mad, are you?' she blurted.

'Mad? No! I'm just glad you're both OK,' he replied. 'And anyway, you missed school to go to a history museum, Claire,' he laughed. 'Don't EVER do it again though,' he added.

'Phew! Sorry, Dad. Honestly, I am,' she said **sincerely**.

Vince's voice lifted. 'Jayne?'

'Yes, darling?'

'Dee's at home, **distraught**. Could you drop Claire there, please? Rebecca's going to be fine; she'll need lots of fluid and rest. There is some **justice** though – the police have arrested that **revolting** boy Drane.'

'Yes, of course, no problem,' replied Jayne. 'I'll drop her off; then I'll message you.'

'Great. See you in a bit, then.'

'Bye, Dad,' Claire shouted.

*

They were almost home; Chorlton wasn't far from town, though the rush hour commuters **congested** the roads into an irritating **gridlock**. Claire peered through the window, finding some **solace** in Drane's arrest, and trying to make sense of the day. Too tired and hungry to think **coherently**, she tipped her head back against the headrest and closed her eyes.

'Penny for those thoughts?' Jayne asked, nudging Claire's arm as they sat in traffic.

'I'm thinking of school on Monday,' she answered. 'I hope they don't **expel** me.' Horrified at the thought, she turned an anguished face towards Jayne.

'Of course they won't. You're hardly a **serial offender**, and it's a history museum, not a nightclub. Still, I guess you're **liable** to be in some trouble,' she added, throwing Claire a **rueful** glance.

In truth, Claire wasn't concerned about school; it **paled** into insignificance right now. That image of Gwilym turning emerald and shattering as that woman plucked the gem from the gold dominated her thoughts.

I must see Gladys, she thought. *My mum's bound to ground me tonight, but I hope she lets me out this weekend*, she worried, not convinced she would.

'Pretty much home now,' said Jayne as they turned onto Barlow Moor Road. 'Not going to spill the beans about today, then?' she asked Claire with a grin.

'It's nothing really. That rat-boy Josh Drane wouldn't let go of Becca, so I **clouted** him,' Claire replied, being **economical** with the truth.

'Wow, Claire, that was brave, but a bit risky. What if he'd hurt you? You won't do that again, will you?' she said with a serious shake of her head.

'No,' replied Claire. 'I acted without thinking.' *It's a half-truth*, she thought guiltily, grimacing at the queues of traffic gassing the air.

She thought of how she'd escaped the boy in the woods and kicked Drane so accurately. She'd not heard anyone else's thoughts since being outside the office, and now she wasn't sure she ever had. But what if these were her talents that Gwilym had **alluded** to? What if she could actually do those things again? Even though everything had dimmed into a hazy blur, she held on to that thought as hard as she could. Besides, even if she could tell Jayne the real story, Jayne would think she was bonkers.

'Course I won't do it again,' Claire reiterated, her eyes angled downwards, looking at her twiddling fingers, which she had crossed as she spoke. She'd never been the best liar.

They drove into Beech Road, and Claire felt sick in anticipation. Her mum would flip! Rain began to pelt down onto the roof as they indicated to pull in and stopped outside Claire's house, Jayne's **automatic ignition** switching off.

1 Why was Claire's father not upset by her actions?

A. He wasn't paying attention to details.

B. He was happy that Claire was fine.

C. He couldn't stay away from work for long.

D. He decided Claire was old enough to look after herself.

2 Which word tells us that Claire's mother was greatly upset?

A. 'sincerely'

B. 'darling'

C. 'distraught'

D. 'revolting'

3 What are 'rush hour commuters'? (line 13)

A. people who drive very fast

B. people who only have one hour to do something

C. people who travel at the busiest time of day

D. people who are in no hurry to get anywhere

4 What word tells us that Claire's father does not like Drane?

A. 'offender'

B. 'expel'

C. 'justice'

D. 'revolting'

5 Why did Claire find 'solace in Drane's arrest' (line 14)?

A. The thought of Drane being under arrest offered Claire some comfort.

B. The idea that Drane was still on the loose bothered her.

C. She was sure that Drane was going to jail.

D. She was comforted by the thought of being away from school.

6 What term from the text means 'someone who repeatedly does the same crime'?

A. 'revolting boy'

B. 'irritating gridlock'

C. 'serial offender'

D. 'anguished face'

7 What does the verb 'pale' mean in the context of this passage?

A. to appear to be less important by comparison

B. to become lighter in complexion

C. to put water into buckets

D. to become friends with someone

8 Find the idiom that means 'to divulge sensitive information'.

A. 'bound to ground'

B. 'pretty much'

C. 'spill the beans'

D. 'being economical with the truth'

9 Which of these words is closest in meaning to 'half-truth', as used on line 33?

A. fabrication

B. hesitation

C. admiration

D. explanation

10 Why did Claire look down at her 'twiddling fingers' (lines 40-41) when talking to Jayne?

A. Claire was thinking very hard about something.

B. She was considering leaving home.

C. She was telling a lie.

D. She was trying to say things in a way that Jayne would understand.

SECTION 2 – CHANGE ONE LETTER

Change just one letter in the word on the left to create a new word that matches the description given.

11	flushing	showing shyness or embarrassment	____________
12	align	unfamiliar, strange or unusual	____________
13	crab	to fill to the point of overflowing	____________
14	mute	to ask oneself in a thoughtful manner	____________
15	stick	done in an impressive and efficient way	____________

SECTION 3 – PARTIAL WORDS

Work out the missing letters to complete the word – a definition of each word is given.

16	O _ T O _ _ N A R _ _ N	a person who is between 80 and 89 years old
17	R U _ _ L _	to mess up something or someone's hair
18	C R _ A _	to make a hoarse, rasping sound when speaking
19	_ _ S C H _ _ _	harm caused by someone or something
20	D _ _ _	flat part of a skateboard or snowboard

SECTION 4 – CLOZE

Fill in the missing letters to complete the passage below.

A	B	C	D	E
retraced	melodic	pinpoint	languid	unison

As the two knights left the museum, a faint crinkle of an echo followed them, its cheerful, **21** ________ notes drifting in waves across the empty hall, akin to wind chimes tinkling in **22** ________ as if pushed by a **23** ________ summer breeze. A smell of fresh lilies swirled upwards, once again filling the air with sweet perfume. Then slowly, one by one, every crack, every split, every fissure in the glass case **24** ________ its original tracks with **25** ________ mathematical precision, until there were none.

SECTION 5 – PARTIAL ANTONYMS

Select the correct combination of letters to complete the antonym of the word on the left.

26 atrocious: g l _ r i _ _ s

A. uou	B. euo	C. aue	D. oou	E. ini

27 remote: i _ _ i n _ n t

A. nne	B. mme	C. spa	D. vao	E. moa

28 board: d _ s _ m b a _ k

A. ues	B. eel	C. ohn	D. aai	E. ier

29 calm: b r i _ _ _ e

A. nkl	B. ttl	C. stl	D. nte	E. mfi

30 apathetic: e n t _ _ s i a s t i _

A. huc	B. rys	C. ele	D. orr	E. euk

REVISION TEST 12

SECTION 1 – LINKED WORDS

Select the word from the options that fits best with the words in both sets of brackets.

1 (example, simulate) (fashion, make-up)

A. characteristic	B. model	C. imitate	D. design	E. style

2 (expensive, sophisticated) (magnificent, impressive)

A. large	B. big	C. tall	D. small	E. grand

3 (terminate, complete) (boundary, limit)

A. border	B. finish	C. alternative	D. end	E. that

4 (love, like) (elaborate, flashy)

A. covet	B. possess	C. fancy	D. lavish	E. classy

5 (aftermath, funeral) (alert, rouse)

A. wake	B. behind	C. consequence	D. surprise	E. trail

SECTION 2 – CLOZE

Choose the most suitable word to fill in the gaps from the corresponding set of brackets.

A	B	C	D	E
memorable	suspects	ordinary	flopped	enjoy

Today, Claire Cadwallader **6** ____________ her surname is the only **7** ____________ thing about her. She thinks she's an **8** ____________ girl whose life is normal. Tonight, she won't do her homework or **9** ____________ her ritual read. Her sneaked snack will go uneaten. She'll fall asleep early, her book **10** ____________ on her chest, her lamp glowing. She's neither tired nor ill. Today is an ordinary day. From tomorrow, Claire will never be the same again.

SECTION 3 – WORD SWAP

Select the two words that need to swap places for the sentence to make sense.

11	A	B	C	D	E	F	G	H
	she	collapsed	to	her	crunch	with	a	knees

12	A	B	C	D	E	F	G	H
	starched	muscles	rippled	discreetly	beneath	his	athletic	shirt

13	A	B	C	D	E	F	G	H
	tilting	his	moment	he	paused	savouring	the	head

14	A	B	C	D	E	F	G	H
	even	its	find	would	struggle	to	maker	it

15	A	B	C	D	E	F	G	H
	what	do	you	old	to	do	intend	friend

SECTION 4 – SYNONYMS

Select the word from the options that is closest in meaning to the word in **bold** on the left.

16	**extravagant**	A. crazy	B. unreasonable	C. spendthrift	D. thrifty
17	**opulence**	A. prosperity	B. simplicity	C. pretentiousness	D. luxuriousness
18	**erratic**	A. compatible	B. inconsistent	C. contradictory	D. consistent
19	**rapturous**	A. ecstatic	B. disconsolate	C. contented	D. cheerful
20	**extortionate**	A. evil	B. monstrous	C. exorbitant	D. competitive

REVISION TEST 13

SECTION 1 – COMPREHENSION

Read the passage and answer the questions that follow.

an extract from The Cadwaladr Quests – Tangled Time – Chapter 19. **The Flying Sponge**

'Come on, spit it out,' Pete said. 'What really went on yesterday with you and Drane at that museum? I know you're not telling all,' Pete asked, squinting at her.

'I am; I have,' she answered in too **shrill** a voice. 'Honestly, I just got lucky. I saw red and shoved Drane as hard as I could. He must have hit his head when he landed or something, and he let go of Becs. Honestly, Pete, it's nothing more than that. How could it be? I'm hardly tiny though, am I? Let's face it, I **bowled** him over with a fair bit of **heft** and a lot of luck,' she finished, avoiding all eye contact with her brother.

Claire hurried her breakfast – Ben would be calling for her at nine-ish. She quickly finished her cereal and rinsed out her bowl and spoon.

'One day, I'm buying Mum a dishwasher,' she said to Pete.

'No room,' drawled Pete, his mouth full. 'And anyway, no need, Eclair – we've got you,' he added, ducking the wet sponge she threw at him. It narrowly missed Pete but hit Dee, who had just walked through the kitchen door.

'Oh, Mum, I'm so sorry,' Claire gasped, her hand over her mouth. The square yellow sponge, like a Post-it note, had stuck to the front of Dee's fluffy dressing gown before plopping to the floor.

A silence fell as Claire and Pete exchanged glances; Dee had not had her coffee yet – this did not **bode** well.

Dee's face was unreadable; then, uncharacteristically, she burst out laughing. Both her kids exhaled in relieved sighs.

'Phew, you were lucky!' Pete whispered out of the corner of his mouth as he squashed past Claire to leave.

'Hey, where are you going, laddie?' asked Dee, back to her normal self in a flash. 'Bowl!' she said, pointing to his **detritus** on the table. 'Sink!' she ordered. 'And don't expect Claire to clear up after you – she's not Cinderella,' added Dee, much to Claire's amusement.

'Nah, but she's got an ugly sister,' retorted Pete in Claire's ear.

Claire laughed out loud, hoping her mum hadn't heard, especially given the state Rebecca had come home in last night.

'How are *you* this morning, Claire, love?' asked Dee.

'I'm fine, Mum. Is Becs OK?'

'She seems to be,' replied Dee. 'She slept well, but then she would do, wouldn't she, drugged up to the eyeballs by that boy?' she finished.

'I'm so glad she's OK, Mum. I really am. I need to rush now though, if you still don't mind,' replied Claire, swiftly closing down the **oncoming debriefing**.

'Rush?' asked Dee.

'I've got Ben's competition,' answered Claire **breezily**, but holding her breath again, silently praying her mum would still let her go.

'Oh yes,' replied Dee. 'But make sure the **snobby** Brady Bunch let me know EXACTLY what time you'll be home, won't you?' sniped Dee, true to form.

'Course, Mum,' laughed Claire. 'They're hardly **snobs** though, Mum. They wouldn't bother with me if they were snobbish, would they?' she said as she left the kitchen and closed the door behind her, hoping her **quip** wasn't a step too far.

Halfway up the stairs, she shouted, 'Oh, Mum, don't forget I'm out with Dad and Jayne tomorrow too,' and with that, she ran up the rest of them before Dee could answer.

1 Find the phrase from the passage that means 'tell the truth quickly'.

A. 'I just got lucky'

B. 'you're not telling all'

C. 'what really went on'

D. 'spit it out'

2 What did Claire mean when she said she 'saw red' (line 3)?

A. She blacked out.

B. She was filled with rage.

C. She noticed the colour red more clearly.

D. She was dizzy.

3 What physical clue did Claire give to show she was not telling everything?

A. She paced restlessly.

B. She kept on looking away.

C. She spoke in a voice that was too high-pitched.

D. She tried to divert attention away from the question.

4 What sporting term did Claire use to describe how she defeated Drane?

A. 'hurried'

B. 'bowled'

C. 'heft'

D. 'threw'

5 What unexpected change occurred concerning Dee?

A. She was expected to be miserable but appeared to be cheerful.

B. She woke up happy but became upset very easily.

C. She told Claire and Pete that she was taking them out for the day.

D. She ran out of the house in a panic.

6 How is emphasis given to the fact that Dee was asking Claire about how she felt?

A. The word 'you' is stressed in italics.

B. Dee calls Claire by her name.

C. An affectionate term, 'love', is used.

D. It is posed as a question.

7 'Becs' (line 29) is an example of ...

A. a misnomer

B. a nickname

C. slang

D. an inside joke

8 What is a 'debriefing' (line 33)?

A. a change of clothes

B. an unpacking of briefcases

C. a verbal punishment for bad behaviour

D. an interview regarding a completed mission

9 Why is the word 'EXACTLY' (line 37) written in upper case when Dee said she wanted Ben's family to let her know when Claire would be home?

A. It is to show that Dee was shouting.

B. It is to show that Dee was placing great emphasis on this particular detail.

C. It is to show that Dee was spelling the word.

D. It is to show that Dee was repeating the word for Claire to hear.

10 How is it emphasised that Rebecca was heavily drugged?

A. It is mentioned that she came home in a 'state'.

B. Obvious disdain is shown towards Drane.

C. The phrase 'up to the eyeballs' is used.

D. It is said that she had slept well.

SECTION 2 – RHYMING

Find a word that rhymes with the word on the left to complete the sentence.

11	ABDICATION	Evans acted without H _ _ I T _ T _ O N.
12	PLATELET	They placed the B _ _ C E _ _ T in the case.
13	SLIDE	Claire felt a huge rush of P _ _ D E.
14	CONDENSATION	Gladys said, 'You have no O B _ I _ A _ _ O N to us.'
15	RECONDITIONED	The Sea King is a D _ C O _ M _ _ S I _ _ E D aircraft.

SECTION 3 – WORD SWAP

Select the two words that need to swap places for the sentence to make sense.

16

A	B	C	D	E	F	G	H
Jack	pulled	away	him	lead	dangling	behind	his

17

A	B	C	D	E	F	G	H
Claire	plonked	herself	hard	on	the	down	bench

18

A	B	C	D	E	F	G	H
the	woman	took	down	and	reached	a	blanket

19

A	B	C	D	E	F	G	H
we'll	our	this	over	put	feet	and	knees

20

A	B	C	D	E	F	G	H
bridge	a	bit	draughty	especially	on	the	gets

SECTION 4 – SYNONYM GROUPS

Which of these groups of words are the most similar in meaning?

21

A. awaken, stir, evoke, arouse

B. basically, lever, dispirit, spark

C. wish, hesitation, utter, streak

D. roll, yank, career, tug

E. retain, sweet, hurtle, perturb

22

A. dilate, clear, splay, spray

B. worry, unease, animal, snozzle

C. jaunty, hazy, full, broad

D. calm, subdue, still, quieten

E. intelligent, reluctant, averse, dark

23

A. conceited, arrogant, egotistical, humble

B. occupant, resident, botany, herbage

C. stoop, hunch, crouch, bend

D. lattice, dubious, endless, network

E. bolt, mimic, post, simulate

24
A. hustle, scoot, fly, career
B. ceaseless, dawdle, temporary, glint
C. post, tower, column, convinced
D. forth, unearth, ahead, forage
E. blithe, breezy, gleam, disbelieving

25
A. tear, pelt, streak, rip
B. haul, advance, scrub, brush
C. bough, fork, foliage, travel
D. dreadful, entwine, knit, mesh
E. gradual, subtle, faint, obvious

SECTION 5 – ADJECTIVES

Select the noun from the options that most closely relates to the adjective in **bold**.

26 **joyful**

A. skin	B. boundary	C. mist	D. expression	E. vision

27 **narrow**

A. region	B. town	C. street	D. county	E. suburb

28 **faithful**

A. hangar	B. yonder	C. legend	D. friend	E. folk

29 **ripe**

A. sausage	B. banana	C. potato	D. cactus	E. bonbon

30 **flashy**

A. smile	B. smoke	C. mass	D. grime	E. skyline

REVISION TEST 14 

SECTION 1 – MISSING LETTERS

Find the letters that have been removed from the word in CAPITALS. Once these letters are placed back in the word, the sentence will make sense.

1 They were en route to a museum, SUPDLY to help with their exam.

A. ossi	B. pose	C. osed	D. arno

2 Rebecca was SURED by a gang of doting admirers.

A. rundo	B. norud	C. droun	D. round

3 He wore banned DEER trainers.

A. igsn	B. gisn	C. sign	D. snig

4 REED by her, he felt his skin crawl as she gnawed the grey gum.

A. puls	B. sulp	C. splu	D. slup

5 Her PATIC, bovine expression reminded him of a cow chewing the cud.

A. hte	B. eth	C. teh	D. het

SECTION 2 – JUMBLED PARAGRAPHS

Choose the most logical order of sentences to construct a meaningful paragraph.

6
a) Dazed and in a stupefied heap, a brilliant flash blinded him.
b) Strips of incandescent light flooded the passage.
c) He fell with a deafening crack and was propelled backwards.
d) His back smacked into the wall.

A. dcba	B. abcd	C. cdab	D. abdc

7
a) He hurled himself head first at the intersecting lasers.
b) The vortex sucked him through the door.
c) He summoned his last drop of physical and mental strength.
d) As his feet left the ground, he flew through the lasers like a rag doll.

A. dcab	B. cadb	C. adcb	D. bacd

8
a) Evans watched helplessly as the Master's eyes swept the room.
b) Dewi, the Master, stood in the doorway.
c) When he saw Dewi in the doorway, he knew it was all over.
d) Dewi took a menacing stride towards him, his eyes taking everything in as he moved forward.

A. cdba	B. acdb	C. dacb	D. bcda

9 a) All this ensured the future talent of his company.

b) If a candidate passed the intelligence tests, state-of-the-art accommodation came with the lucrative salary.

c) Flaunting an audacious self-belief, Lewis had brazenly constructed futuristic offices.

d) He constructed them in obscure, deprived areas, bypassing the predictable, affluent towns.

A. cdba	B. badc	C. dacb	D. adcb

10 a) Blinking madly, he blew through cracked lips, trying to fan them away.

b) The faster he blew, the more his head whirled and buzzed.

c) A multitude of legs tickled and irritated him intensely.

d) Unable to move, he winced as an army of ants marched across his cheeks.

A. dbca	B. bcad	C. dcab	D. abcd

SECTION 3 – VOCABULARY IN CONTEXT

Select the most appropriate option that matches the meaning of the word underlined in the sentence.

11 **Straining her neck, she turned back, savouring one last look at the memorable scene.**

A. She turned around so fast that she strained her neck.

B. Before she turned to go back, she took a final look at the view.

C. Before the view disappeared, she stretched around to take a final long look at the scene.

D. The scene was so amazing that she got a crick in her neck looking at it.

E. She had to turn away from gazing at the view because her neck was sore.

12 **'She banished her woes and enjoyed the journey'.**

A. She commanded her woes to disappear.

B. She put her troubles to the back of her mind in the meantime.

C. She spent half the time enjoying the journey and the other half nursing her woes.

D. The excitement of the journey made her completely forget her troubles.

E. She enjoyed worrying about her troubles throughout the journey.

13 **The bikers weren't moving forward or overtaking; instead, they drove precariously close to the pony trap.**

A. The bikers accidentally came too close to the pony trap.

B. The bikers were unable to go faster than the pony trap and came rather too close.

C. The bikers showed off their amazing skills by driving as close as possible to the pony trap.

D. The pony trap was so wide the bikers couldn't overtake and ended up closer than they intended.

E. The bikers kept pace with the pony trap and drove dangerously near to it.

14 **'The road was flanked on both sides by flat fields.'**

A. The road was built up on a platform alongside the fields.

B. The road had fields to either side of it.

C. The road was separated from the fields by a ditch on both sides.

D. The road was fenced off from the fields on each side.

E. There was no barrier between the road and the fields.

15 'Warning lights flashed <u>intermittently</u> red.'

A. The red warning lights flashed on and off sporadically.

B. The warning lights stayed on red for what seemed like forever.

C. The red warning lights continually flashed on and off.

D. There was an occasional flash of red warning lights.

E. The warning lights alternated between red and other colours.

SECTION 4 – ODD WORD OUT

Select the odd word out in each set of words.

16	A. crude	B. permanent	C. makeshift	D. improvised
17	A. inept	B. clumsy	C. awkward	D. adroit
18	A. ordinary	B. quaint	C. charming	D. appealing
19	A. baffle	B. clarify	C. perplex	D. puzzle
20	A. exciting	B. intoxicating	C. thrilling	D. boring

REVISION TEST 15

SECTION 1 – COMPREHENSION

Read the passage and answer the questions that follow.

an extract from The Cadwaladr Quests – Tangled Time – Chapter 3. **An Old Betrayal**

The **colossal** man driving the trap remained silent, staring **steadfastly** ahead with his **canine** co-driver. He clucked an occasional sound **encouraging** the pony's pace to pick up, but nothing more.

His **sculpted, chiselled** features glowed a **ruddy** red, and his hands, the size of shovels, were tinged a purple hue in the chilly air. His Roman nose jutted out from his face at a proud angle above weathered skin mapped with **intricate** veins and **craggy etchings**. His full mouth and lips **divulged** no **emotion**. Claire guessed he might be a farmer; his **tweed** clothes and flat cap looked well-worn and in need of a wash. Despite his frayed **attire**, he exuded an **indescribable** air. Claire imagined he'd **tolerate** little nonsense. Jack hadn't **budged** an inch from this solid man's lap during the entire journey.

Claire's **equine** experience **amounted to** nothing, yet she found this **unforeseen** ride **exhilarating**. The pony's coat was the colour of Victorian red brick, yet gleamed as richly as a **buffed**, polished chestnut. A muscular, arched neck held a proud, pretty head crowned nobly by a long sandy mane. This soft cream trim matched the silken tail, whose flowing ribbons of hair billowed in the wind. **Soothed** by the simple rhythmic clip-clop of hooves on the road, her spirits lifted a touch.

So much nicer than cars, she thought as the trap bumped along the deserted road. *But where are all the cars?* she wondered. It struck her that none had overtaken them. *How weird! Is Wales always this quiet?* she asked herself.

The road narrowed; a **sinister** dusk fell as **gnarled**, twisted trees lined and **canopied** their way. The trap's wheels sank into deep **potholes**, squirting sloppy mud up the sides, spraying the passengers. Claire rubbed at her mouth, spitting out specks of gritty dirt.

As quickly as it had narrowed, the road widened and eased. She stretched her cold, stiff fingers, **kneading** some life back into her creaky white knuckles. Without moving her head, she swivelled her eyes and sneaked a **furtive** glance at the two strangers.

1 Which word tells us the driver is not small or medium in size?

A. 'colossal'

B. 'chiselled'

C. 'steadfastly'

D. 'craggy'

2 What is the 'trap' that the man was driving?

A. a train

B. a tram

C. a car

D. a carriage

3 How did the man make the pony go faster?

A. He used a whip.

B. He made a clucking sound.

C. He shouted at it.

D. He held a carrot in front of it.

4 Which two words in the second paragraph tell us the driver has a well-defined face?

A. 'ruddy' and 'purple'

B. 'tinged' and 'divulged'

C. 'intricate' and 'craggy'

D. 'sculpted' and 'chiselled'

5 How do we know the driver probably spent a lot of time outside in harsh conditions?

A. He has a full mouth and lips.

B. His face is weathered.

C. His hands are as big as shovels.

D. He has an aquiline nose.

6 What is meant by 'his full mouth and lips divulged no emotion' (line 5)?

A. He was busy eating.

B. It was impossible to tell his mood.

C. He didn't talk much.

D. He was good at keeping secrets.

7 Find the word that means 'of or related to horses'.

A. 'tolerate'

B. 'budged'

C. 'equine'

D. 'ride'

8 What did Claire find unusual on her journey?

A. There were no cars.

B. There were too many people.

C. The sun wasn't shining.

D. There were no phones.

9 'Clip-clop' (line 13) is an example of ...

A. idiomatic expression

B. symbolism

C. onomatopoeia

D. surrealism

10 Claire seemed to have mixed emotions about her journey so far. What were they?

A. relaxed but worried

B. exhilarated but anxious

C. calm but queer

D. sad but optimistic

SECTION 2 – SPELLING ERRORS

Select the word in each group that has not been spelled correctly.

11	A. elevated	B. raised	C. promoted	D. advansed	E. upgraded
12	A. voyager	B. sightseer	C. traveller	D. comutter	E. passenger
13	A. irresistable	B. enticing	C. tantalising	D. unappealing	E. attractive
14	A. strengthened	B. amplified	C. intensified	D. increased	E. hieghtened
15	A. solemn	B. funeral	C. mournful	D. melancholy	E. somber

SECTION 3 – WORD DEFINITIONS

Select the definition that best suits the word.

16 'inspection'

A. to dive into

B. inward looking

C. careful examination or scrutiny

D. reconsideration

E. in particular, specifically

17 'heirloom'

A. a monetary endowment

B. a loom for weaving hair

C. an item inherited from ancestors

D. a legal settlement figure

E. a pedigree certificate

18 'flamboyant'

A. flammable and unsinkable

B. showy and extravagant

C. shy and retiring

D. a fierce type of male ant

E. brilliant, eye-catching colour

19 'reserve'

A. to keep something aside for later use

B. a term used for ancestral property

C. postponing something

D. an area of land allocated for special purposes

E. a predisposition to reticence

20 'despise'

A. to express a prejudicial opinion

B. to take offence at something

C. to show an inflexible attitude

D. a negative reaction to food

E. to view with contempt

SECTION 4 – SYNONYMS

Select the word from the options that is closest in meaning to the word in **bold** on the left.

21	**core**	A. apple	B. centre	C. circumference	D. diameter
22	**witness**	A. observer	B. blogger	C. rubberneck	D. victim
23	**unavoidable**	A. suggested	B. preventable	C. predestined	D. inescapable
24	**submissive**	A. humble	B. reverent	C. compliant	D. dedicated
25	**towering**	A. cosmic	B. high	C. prodigious	D. weighty

SECTION 5 – SHUFFLED SENTENCES

Rearrange the words to form a meaningful sentence and find the superfluous word.

26 the skip Jack scaled steep steps a time two at

27 gullible her fallen down for had sister Josh Drane

28 my you master says you reap kung fu sow in this what you world

29 she never invitation took the for granted super

30 Claire in the the hall bag left her

REVISION TEST 16

SECTION 1 – ADJECTIVES

Select the noun from the options that most closely relates to the adjective in **bold**.

1 **pulpy**

A. noise	B. writing	C. dog	D. earth	E. powder

2 **gruelling**

A. pot	B. exercise	C. machine	D. look	E. person

3 **smarting**

A. brain	B. advert	C. rain	D. sweets	E. pain

4 **unrelenting**

A. grip	B. trip	C. ship	D. book	E. man

5 **credible**

A. tape	B. teeth	C. biscuit	D. story	E. luck

SECTION 2 – HOMOPHONES

Choose the word that corresponds to the correct spelling for the given definition.

6	to cry profusely	wail	whale
7	to forgo a right	waive	wave
8	a piece on a chessboard	knight	night
9	the flesh of an animal	meet	meat
10	stretched or pulled tight	taut	taught

SECTION 3 – LINKED WORDS

Select the word from the options that fits best with the words in both sets of brackets.

11 (complement, enhance) (tuxedo, formal)

A. supplement	B. augment	C. suit	D. party	E. ball

12 (rational, coherent) (vivid, explicit)

A. opaque	B. simple	C. lucid	D. luminous	E. wise

13 (rugged, strong) (rich, flavourful)

A. robust	B. rough	C. meaty	D. craggy	E. harsh

14	(subtle, pastel)			(ashen, pasty)	
	A. ghostly	B. faded	C. pale	D. rosiness	E. yellow

15	(persuasive, suave)			(deceptive, manipulative)	
	A. beguiling	B. foxy	C. credible	D. intelligent	E. convincing

SECTION 4 – CLOZE

Use the highlighted words from the passage to complete the following sentences.

The familiar museum was **deserted**. There was no sign of Mr or Mrs Evans, who were **supposed** to guard the hallowed bracelet. Where were Gwilym and Owain? Claire **willed** them to appear, to land in the helicopter she had waved them off in just hours before from Gladys Jones's front door. With a **futile** wish, she glanced at the basement door. In **earnest** she hoped that Jack might appear to save the day.

16	'Please say yes,' he said to her, in a very _____________ tone of voice.
17	'You are so strong- _____________,' said Kate. 'I don't know why I married you.'
18	When they got there, the place was completely _____________.
19	He was _____________ to have arrived by five o'clock.
20	He knew it was _____________ to try to escape, but he bought a ticket to New York anyway.

REVISION TEST 17

SECTION 1 – COMPREHENSION

Read the passage and answer the questions that follow.

an extract from The Cadwaladr Quests – Tangled Time – Chapter 13. **Exhibition Case 111**

Even in **shapeless** fluorescent work **garments**, Felicity's prettiness shone. 'Yes. We'll meet you there, Flic,' replied Gwilym, using her **abbreviated** name.

The vast exhibition hall had finally been **evacuated** and the alarms switched off. **Dopey** Dave and blundering Bert had slouched off upstairs and were back to normal, stuffing down popcorn and **guffawing** at a movie. After all, the police were in charge now.

Owain approached a solitary Gwilym, who now stood by the cracked case. 'Sir, I sense your unease and **preoccupation** towards the **fledgling** Instinctive.'

'I hope she is **resourceful**.' Gwilym frowned as he spoke to Owain. 'She is faced with such **onerous adversity** so soon.'

'She has already begun to prove herself,' replied Owain, touching Gwilym's shoulder. 'You are **weary**, my friend.'

'Yes, perhaps I am a little tired,' replied Gwilym as they walked across the hall, approaching Mrs Evans still sitting in the office chair.

'Marjorie, how are you now?'

'I am fine now, sir,' she replied. 'Do we have any word from Robert? Do we know if the Cutter is safe?' As she spoke, her **taut** skin pulled over her **skeletal** cheekbones and ashen face. Her **hollow** voice faltered to a mere croak, barely audible even in the small office.

Gwilym watched her; she appeared changed, **sunken** with **fretfulness** and **fatigue**.

'Not yet, though no doubt we will soon,' he responded. 'You must rest, Marjorie. Close the museum for a while and wait for him. If he contacts us first, we will let you know,' said Gwilym, encouraging her as he spoke.

'Yes, sir. Of course, you are right,' she **concurred**.

Concerned, Gwilym watched her get up and **hobble** away, her gait stiff and laborious, but they must leave her.

'Come, Owain,' beckoned Gwilym. 'We still have work to do.'

As the two knights left the museum, a faint crinkle of an echo followed them, its cheerful, **melodic** notes drifting in waves across the empty hall, akin to wind chimes tinkling in **unison** as if pushed by a **languid** summer breeze. A smell of fresh lilies swirled upwards, once again filling the air with sweet perfume. Then slowly, one by one, every crack, every split, every fissure in the glass case **retraced** its original tracks with **pinpoint** mathematical precision, until there were none.

Case 111 looked exactly as it had that morning.

1 **What positive contradiction is observed regarding Felicity?**

A. Her friends call her Flic.

B. She is beautiful even in work clothes.

C. She is unusually tall.

D. She appears to be beautiful but speaks in an unattractive manner.

2 **What is 'Flic' (line 1) an example of?**

A. a pseudonym

B. a nom de plume

C. a nom de guerre

D. a shortened name

3 'Dopey Dave' (line 3) is an example of ...

A. a joke

B. a famous name

C. vernacular

D. a derogatory term

4 What was Dave and Bert's usual behaviour?

A. They watched the security cameras for any unusual behaviour.

B. They ate popcorn and watched movies.

C. They played cards.

D. They listened to the radio.

5 Why were Dave and Bert no longer concerned?

A. The threat had been averted.

B. The police had caught the thief.

C. The police were in charge.

D. It was a false alarm.

6 Which word in lines 6 to 7 tells us that Gwilym was alone?

A. 'solitary'

B. 'unease'

C. 'preoccupation'

D. 'fledgling'

7 Which word in lines 16 to 17 tells us that Marjorie is extremely thin?

A. 'skeletal'

B. 'hollow'

C. 'croak'

D. 'mere'

8 What advice did Gwilym give Marjorie?

A. He suggested that Marjorie has a rest.

B. He suggested that Marjorie stays vigilant.

C. He suggested that Marjorie goes on holiday.

D. He suggested that Marjorie takes medicine.

9 What is the sound of exhibition case 111 repairing itself likened to?

A. wind chimes in a rough wind

B. wind chimes in a summer storm

C. wind chimes in a languid summer breeze

D. wind chimes in a tranquil spring breeze

10 Considering the repair done to exhibition case 111, what can we assume about Dewi's plan?

A. His plan was a success.

B. His plan had failed.

C. He was going to return.

D. He had been betrayed.

SECTION 2 – SPELLING ERRORS

Select the word in each group that has not been spelled correctly.

11	A. compell	B. jut	C. tremor	D. fabric	E. velvety
12	A. buff	B. almond	C. constant	D. consistant	E. camel
13	A. reticent	B. cagey	C. gaurded	D. easily	E. textile
14	A. abcense	B. rough	C. coarse	D. dye	E. pigment
15	A. delicately	B. enormity	C. haste	D. jepoardy	E. attendance

Section 3 – ANAGRAMS

Rearrange the letters of the word on the left to make a suitable word for the sentence on the right.

16	FRINGES	She crossed her ☐☐☐☐☐☐☐ and sat down.
17	CURBS	The walls needed a proper ☐☐☐☐☐ .
18	FROWARD	They settled into a ☐☐☐☐☐☐☐ -facing window seat.
19	DROLLEST	An elderly woman ☐☐☐☐☐☐☐☐ down the aisle.
20	GAPES	She thumbed through the ☐☐☐☐☐ .

SECTION 4 – ANTONYMS

Choose the word that is most opposite to the word on the left.

21	charming	A. violent	B. pleasant	C. repulsive	D. delightful
22	latter	A. former	B. primordial	C. hindmost	D. final
23	humble	A. unassertive	B. unostentatious	C. proud	D. extrovert
24	persistent	A. patient	B. sustained	C. intermittent	D. cyclic
25	wake	A. doze	B. rouse	C. inspire	D. sleep

SECTION 5 – CHANGE ONE LETTER

Change just one letter in the word on the left to create a new word that matches the description given.

26	stomp	to bend one's head or body downwards	________
27	speak	a tiny spot or particle	________
28	bevy	to impose a tax, fee or fine	________
29	dense	the faculty by which the body perceives an external stimulus	________
30	chamber	to climb or move in an awkward or laborious way	________

REVISION TEST 18 

SECTION 1 – ODD WORD OUT

Select the odd word out in each set of words.

1	A. exasperated	B. pleased	C. agitated	D. annoyed	E. frustrated
2	A. destitute	B. prosperous	C. comfortable	D. rich	E. wealthy
3	A. contemporary	B. current	C. new	D. outmoded	E. fashionable
4	A. sincere	B. straightforward	C. candid	D. sarcastic	E. honest
5	A. remodel	B. alter	C. convert	D. preserve	E. modify

SECTION 2 – SYNONYMS

Select the word from the options that is closest in meaning to the word in **bold** on the left.

6	**inconsolable**	A. undulating	B. uncomfortable	C. heartbroken	D. sickened
7	**incessant**	A. ceaseless	B. unchaste	C. interrupted	D. eternal
8	**lunged**	A. expired	B. oxygenated	C. shoved	D. thrusted
9	**involuntary**	A. reflexive	B. willing	C. deliberate	D. prescribed
10	**careered**	A. determined	B. rushed	C. buzzed	D. bombarded

SECTION 3 – CLOZE

Fill in the missing letters to complete the passage below.

They'd booked an **11** e _ p _ _ s i _ e restaurant too; she might even be reduced to **12** s c _ _ u n _ _ _ g clothes from Rebecca. Claire's **13** _ a r _ _ o b _ consisted of jeans, hoodies and **14** _ _ a i _ _ _ s.

'Can't work out what Princess Jayne sees in your dad,' her mum would **15** s _ i p _.

SECTION 4 – PARTIAL WORDS

Work out the missing letters to complete the word – a definition of each word is given.

16	H _ R _ _ _ C	having brave and courageous characteristics
17	I M _ U L _ _ V _	done without thinking about beforehand
18	_ _ L A T _ _ E	displaying random and quick changes of emotion
19	S _ L _ _ _ H	lacking consideration for others
20	S E _ _ E S _ _ R	to keep apart, or to hide away from

REVISION TEST 19

SECTION 1 – COMPREHENSION

Read the passage and answer the questions that follow.

an extract from The Cadwaladr Quests – Tangled Time – Chapter 17. **How Evans Tangled Time Alone**

Whilst Claire slept at home, more truth to the story unfolded deep in the underground tunnels.

Busy foraging for food in the damp black recess, beetles, bugs and insects scurried about their daily **duties**. A **swollen** cocoa-brown **cockroach deposited** her precious eggs in the peaceful, moist crevice she had **fortuitously** discovered in the nook behind the man's knees. This unusual **incubator** had lain still long enough to present her with the ideal **hatching** place for her egg case, although she didn't realise her eggs would never quite reach the forty-something days required for **maturation**.

Like a full-term **babe cocooned** in its mother's **womb**, Robert Evans lay still, curled up in the soggy soil, bent knees pulled up close, locked to his chest, small, **petulant** fists tucked away in angry balls above them. His bony, bare feet protruded from shredded trousers, and a scant, **ragged** shirt partially exposed the **sullied** dirty-white skin on his arms. A neat black beaver-cloth **waistcoat**, **intact** and still buttoned, had endured the ordeal. **Prim** and **incongruous**, it **swaddled** his upper **torso** as if he were **aptly** dressed for a morning at church.

Silent and still, he appeared at peace. Sleeping, perhaps. However, this **refuge** offered little **nurturing**. No such loving, **matriarchal** comfort blanket existed here.

How long he had **languished** there, dormant, was difficult to **gauge**. How **injurious** his unpreventable sacrifice would be was not yet apparent, because earlier today this **diminutive** man had surpassed all other Knights Hawk; he had tangled time alone. **Eclipsing** all others, he had reached the **pinnacle** of his **existence** and changed the landscape permanently. Robert Evans hoped his heroic deed would go down in history for **millennia** to come, for in his fist, he still clutched the tiny arrow. One half of the precious Cutter, which he had snatched from the fairy figurine whilst attempting his one desperate hope of escaping his sinister **pursuer** – Dewi, the Master.

1 How is the co-occurrence of events established at the beginning of the passage?

A. Figurative language is used.

B. Prepositions are used.

C. Similes are used in the first few lines.

D. The passage starts with a conjunction.

2 What word in the first five lines tells us that the cockroach found the crevice by chance?

A. 'fortuitously'

B. 'nook'

C. 'unusual'

D. 'ideal'

3 What financial term is used in regard to the cockroach?

A. The cockroach's eggs were 'precious'.

B. The cockroach 'deposited' her eggs.

C. The cockroach had 'fortuitously' discovered the nook.

D. The incubator was 'unusual'.

4 Where did the cockroach lay her eggs?

A. in the nook behind Robert Evans's knees

B. in a crevice in the tunnel walls

C. in a box

D. in a hole in the earth

5 What does the use of 'forty-something' (line 6) tell us about the incubation period of the eggs?

A. The incubation period is less than forty days.

B. The incubation period is over fifty days.

C. The incubation period is exactly forty days.

D. The incubation period is approximately forty days.

6 How is Robert Evans portrayed in the text?

A. He is portrayed in a childlike manner.

B. He is portrayed in a heroic manner.

C. He is portrayed in a serious manner.

D. He is portrayed in a comedic manner.

7 What appeared to be out of place with Robert Evans's appearance?

A. He seemed too serious for the clothes he was wearing.

B. He was clean, but his clothes were dirty.

C. His waistcoat was tidy, but he was dirty.

D. His feet were bare, but his legs were clothed.

8 Select a word from lines 9 to 11 that tells us that Robert Evans was dirty.

A. 'aptly'

B. 'ordeal'

C. 'intact'

D. 'sullied'

9 What does the word 'swaddled' tell us about the waistcoat (line 11)?

A. The waistcoat fitted Robert Evans snugly.

B. The waistcoat was dirty.

C. The waistcoat fitted loosely.

D. The waistcoat was torn.

10 Why is a comparison made to being 'dressed for a morning at church' (lines 11-12)?

A. People are expected to wear old clothes to church.

B. People are expected to wear neat, clean clothes to church.

C. People are expected to wear casual clothes to church.

D. People are expected to wear uniforms to church.

SECTION 2 – LINKED WORDS

Select the word from the options that fits best with the words in both sets of brackets.

11 (sad, forlorn) (injured, broken)

A. cold	B. dinner	C. annoyed	D. hurt	E. killer

12 (stare, glower) (beam, dazzle)

A. frown	B. blaze	C. flame	D. flare	E. glare

13 (stifle, restrain) (quiet, calm)

A. control	B. silence	C. still	D. encourage	E. abandon

14 (devious, cunning) (artistic, creative)

A. clumsy	B. persuasive	C. foxy	D. deceptive	E. crafty

15 (disappear, hide) (dress, enrobe)

A. camouflage	B. costume	C. cloak	D. charade	E. false

SECTION 3 – VOCABULARY IN CONTEXT

Select the most appropriate option that matches the meaning of the word underlined in the sentence.

16 She was completely flummoxed by the simultaneous juxtaposition of the two images.

A. The appearance of the two images made her feel dizzy and light-headed.

B. She was bewildered by both images appearing at the same time.

C. She got into a tizzy because the images upset her equilibrium.

D. When the two images were presented, she felt as if she were floating on air.

E. The appearance together of those two images simply took her breath away.

17 Adjacent to the village green stood a single row of charming Victorian cottages.

A. A row of Victorian cottages had been built around the same time as the village green was made.

B. The Victorian cottages stood quite a distance away from the village green.

C. In the middle of the village green was a single row of Victorian cottages.

D. The Victorian cottages were built alongside the village green.

E. In contrast to the village green, the Victorian cottages were pleasant to behold.

18 The freshly baked bread that Gladys made rivalled Ben's mum's bread.

A. Gladys's bread was every bit as good as the bread baked by Ben's mum.

B. Gladys was trying to outdo Ben's mum by baking even nicer bread.

C. The bread that Gladys baked wasn't a patch on Ben's mum's bread.

D. Gladys's bread was far better than Ben's mum's bread.

E. The bread made by Gladys was almost identical to the bread Ben's mum made.

19 Gladys chided the children because they were feeding Jack titbits.

A. Gladys commended the children for being so kind to Jack.

B. Gladys encouraged the children to give the dog more food.

C. Gladys laughed at the children as they fed the dog.

D. Gladys scolded the children because she didn't want Jack to get titbits.

E. Gladys patted the children tenderly on the back because they loved her dog.

20 Dee had an aversion to animals.

A. Dee imagined that animals were versions of herself.

B. Dee had a special affinity with animals.

C. Dee was allergic to animals.

D. Dee adored animals.

E. Dee had a strong dislike for animals.

SECTION 4 – COMPOUND WORDS

Select the option that forms a compound word once the blank is filled in.

21 **Some**_______ jutted out from underneath.

A. how	B. what	C. thing	D. time

22 A neat buff envelope, beautifully **hand**_______.

A. held	B. cuffed	C. woven	D. written

23 She stuffed the money deep into her **back**_______.

A. pack	B. yard	C. ground	D. side

24 The train clattered through the **out**_______ and on into the city.

A. doors	B. field	C. skirts	D. flow

25 He looked like a Dickensian **under**_______ in his formal black suit and tie.

A. world	B. achiever	C. dog	D. taker

SECTION 5 – HOMOPHONES

From the available choices, select the most appropriate option.

26 She ran _______ an open barrier, taking the stairs _____ at a time.

A. through, too	B. threw, two	C. threw, to	D. through, two

27 Suddenly Jack _______ so hard on his lead that she lost her ______ on him.

A. pulled, holed	B. pooled, hold	C. pulled, hold	D. pooled, holed

28 Claire glanced around, ________ with relief, ______ the boys had gone.

A. week, but	B. weak, but	C. week, butt	D. weak, butt

29 Jack's _______ wagged. 'Look, he _______ me,' she said.

A. tail, knows	B. tail, nose	C. tale, knows	D. tale, nose

30 If asked, she _________ have taken the _______ of the pony trap.

A. wood, reins	B. would, rains	C. wood, rains	D. would, reins

REVISION TEST 20

SECTION 1 – COMPOUND WORDS

Select the option that forms a compound word once the blank is filled in.

1 She can be a bit of an air ________.

A. net	B. head	C. craft	D. bubble

2 Jayne said, 'I won't be judge________, Claire, so tell me what happened.'

A. cerebral	B. intellectual	C. cognitive	D. mental

3 Rush hour commuters caused an irritating grid________.

A. catch	B. lock	C. clasp	D. bolt

4 She tipped her head back against the head________ and closed her eyes.

A. slumber	B. snooze	C. rest	D. sleep

5 The movie clip had broad________ nothing significant.

A. chucked	B. thrown	C. cast	D. lobbed

SECTION 2 – WORD SWAP

Underline the two words that need to swap places in the sentence in order to make sense.

6 Claire foliage wildly at spiky grasped.

7 Gasping, halt slowed to a chaotic she on a slight plateau.

8 He was about to ankles hold of her grab – again.

9 She unrelenting struggling but his grip was stopped.

10 He stared at his with revulsion on her face.

SECTION 3 – REPLACE THE WORD

In each of the following sentences, replace one word with a word from the word bank so that the sentence continues to make sense.

A	B	C	D	E
mess	forlorn	lacklustre	prodded	cranked

11	She turned up the heating.
12	The doughnut sat alone in the bread bin.
13	It's a right tip in there.
14	Tea was uninspiring, as usual.
15	He jabbed at his food with his fork.

SECTION 4 – ANTONYMS

Choose the word that is most opposite to the word on the left.

16	**bland**	A. disagreeable	B. mild	C. pungent	D. fragrant
17	**bewilder**	A. mystify	B. bemuse	C. confound	D. enlighten
18	**inhabit**	A. reside	B. occupy	C. visit	D. dwell
19	**bold**	A. energetic	B. feisty	C. spirited	D. dull
20	**lethargic**	A. torpid	B. inactive	C. spry	D. indolent

REVISION TEST 21

SECTION 1 – COMPREHENSION

Read the passage and answer the questions that follow.

an extract from The Cadwaladr Quests – Tangled Time – Chapter 9. **Hearing Things**

As Claire glanced back at the basement's closed door, she stifled a cough, spluttering as her heart **pummelled** her chest, as if its rhythm was thrown **askew**. Gwilym had pursued the Master, **abandoning** her to **fend for herself**.

So far, unable to move, she'd achieved nothing. Anxiety gnawed her stomach, twisting the emptiness as weakness **consumed** her. She trembled, unable to **assemble** her thoughts.

What had Gwilym said? She tried to remember. **Detached** from reality, she envisaged knights **toiling** in suffocating mines, **sacrificing** everything to find the magical Welsh gold. She pictured Rebecca, her Mum and Dad, Jayne's warm smile and Ben beaming at his winner's medals. Their images **waltzed** in **frivolous merriment**, dizzying her head. Then, reality kicked back in, and cruel, salty tears washed the images clear away, blurring her vision as they did.

This morning she'd been Claire Cadwallader, a schoolgirl. What had she become? Some knight's 'niece' with 'Instinct', capable of remarkable feats? She didn't know, and she didn't believe it, and now she faced an unknown, imminent test – alone.

Managing to take tiny steps, she ducked amongst the exhibits, avoiding being seen by the two security guards at the other end of the hall. One guard held a boy she recognised from Rebecca's year. There was no sign of the rest of Rebecca's class.

She dropped onto all fours and **inched prudently** forward, zigzagging around cabinets and stands, her knees gathering a collection of dusty grit as she crawled across the wide hall towards the office that held her sister. Reaching the other side, she rested against the wall between two shelves, steeling herself to move further along to the office.

Eventually, she broke cover and crawled up close to the office door, her heart beating in her throat. **Paling**, she froze after her shoulder banged hard against the door frame.

'Ow!' She'd bitten her lip so hard it bled. Licking the blood away, she awaited discovery but, thank goodness, none came. Her **knotted** shoulders **slackened** in relief as a long, silent sigh escaped her lungs.

Stalling, consumed by fear and **indecision**, she bit her nails and **vacantly** regarded some ugly vases in a nearby case. She crouched half-upright and turned to face the door that stood between her and Rebecca. **Teetering**, she reached for the handle but, unable to bring herself to turn it, retreated. She leaned back against the wall, **frustrated** and annoyed, and sank down onto her backside. As she landed, she accidentally whipped her head sideways, catching her temple on the doorframe with a thud. It hurt.

'Ouch!' she yelped, rubbing the **sizeable** lump that **instantaneously** popped up.

1 Select the word from the first ten lines that tells us that Claire did not look at the door for long.

A. 'askew'

B. 'frivolous'

C. 'toiling'

D. 'glanced'

2 'Her heart pummelled her chest' (lines 1–2) is an example of which literary device?

A. onomatopoeia

B. personification

C. juxtaposition

D. foreshadowing

3 Find another example of the literary device found as question 2's answer in the first ten lines of the text.

A. 'glanced back at the basement's closed door'

B. 'fend for herself'

C. 'anxiety gnawed her stomach'

D. 'she envisioned knights toiling in suffocating mines'

4 Why did Claire feel defeated?

A. She was hungry and thirsty.

B. She had achieved nothing.

C. She had lost her siblings.

D. She couldn't remember the right path.

5 What is the likely reason for Claire detaching from reality?

A. It is a coping mechanism.

B. It is a way to pass the time.

C. It is a way for her to brainstorm.

D. It is to help organise her thoughts.

6 How had Claire changed between the start of the story and now?

A. She had gone from being a schoolgirl to a blacksmith.

B. She had gone from being a schoolgirl to a knight.

C. She had gone from being a schoolgirl to a knight's niece.

D. She had gone from being a schoolgirl to a sorceress.

7 Why was Claire unsure of herself?

A. She was facing a crisis at home.

B. She was overdue on her homework assignment.

C. She had fallen ill on her adventures.

D. She was facing an uncertain problem by herself.

8 What is meant when it is said that Claire 'inched prudently forward' (line 17)?

A. Claire was moving carefully.

B. Claire was moving confidently.

C. Claire was moving consistently.

D. Claire was moving carelessly.

9 Find a word between lines 20 and 25 that shows that Claire lost colour in her face due to shock.

A. 'vacantly'

B. 'stalling'

C. 'teetering'

D. 'paling'

10 **What visible manifestation of Claire's body relaxing can be seen?**

A. She relaxed her shoulders and stretched.

B. She let out a sigh and stretched.

C. She sat down and yawned.

D. She relaxed her shoulders and let out a sigh.

SECTION 2 – PARTIAL SYNONYMS

Complete the words on the right to form a word that means the same or nearly the same as the word on the left.

11	ETERNALLY	P E _ _ _ T U A _ _ Y
12	SELDOM	_ _ _ E L Y
13	HEED	R E _ _ _ D
14	AVERSION	_ _ _ U G _ _ N C E
15	IMPRESS	I N _ _ I R _

SECTION 3 – SHUFFLED SENTENCES

Rearrange the words to form a meaningful sentence and find the superfluous word.

16	carpet at staring Claire stiffened with the
17	lifted gingerly to avoid more the damage she him
18	sorrow in her face a mixture of love wore and
19	flannel with to wet freezing I'm going this and water
20	she door locked and ducked it through into the bathroom

SECTION 4 – VOCABULARY IN CONTEXT

Select the most appropriate option that matches the meaning of the word underlined in the sentence.

21 **Drane lay nursing his battered leg on the office floor.**

A. Drane was a qualified nurse, and he was therefore able to look after his leg.

B. Someone had deep-fried Drane's leg in batter.

C. Drane was so badly injured he could only lie on the floor and attend to his sore leg.

D. Drane's leg was severed, and he could only watch as it lay on the floor of the office.

E. Drane was trying to protect his wounded leg from becoming contaminated by the dirty floor.

22 **The Master continued to goad and taunt his old adversary Gwilym.**

A. The Master continually said things that he knew would annoy his old enemy.

B. The Master prodded Gwilym with a stick.

C. The Master kept on encouraging Gwilym.

D. The Master wouldn't stop walking round and round his old adversary.

E. Gwilym hated the Master because he kept being so nasty to him.

23 'You were always an <u>insipid</u> fool,' Dewi ridiculed.

A. With his gentle banter, Dewi was actually paying Gwilym a backhanded compliment.

B. Dewi's opinion of Gwilym was that he was a dull and boring dunce.

C. Dewi thought Gwilym was very foolish even though he had always been intelligent.

D. Dewi said that Gwilym was a very brave idiot.

E. Dewi despised Gwilym because he displayed such weakness.

24 Dewi snarled with an <u>outlandish</u> twist of his face.

A. Dewi's face displayed an unfamiliar glow of pleasure.

B. Dewi had a roguish look when he snarled.

C. Dewi's twisted features had the rugged, weather-beaten texture of a landscape.

D. Dewi was so angry his face became contorted.

E. When Dewi snarled, he pushed his face forward aggressively.

25 Drane <u>inadvertently</u> relaxed his grip on Rebecca.

A. Drane was so exhausted he had to let go of Rebecca.

B. Drane deliberately dropped Rebecca.

C. Drane alternated between a tight and weak grip on Rebecca.

D. Drane unintentionally released his hold on Rebecca.

E. Drane reluctantly let go of Rebecca.

SECTION 5 – CLOZE

Choose the word that best completes the sentence.

26 Claire looked from the case to Gwilym, __________ by his apathy.

A. derived	B. lamented	C. evidenced	D. baffled	E. disgraced

27 He __________ his skateboard along with his toe.

A. flattered	B. pushed	C. galloped	D. scratched	E. gathered

28 One of England's most ________ city centres was just down the road.

A. tired	B. placid	C. populous	D. obvious	E. gated

29 Gladys was a _________ and amiable octogenarian.

A. admirable	B. stiff	C. young	D. alien	E. sprightly

30 The knight squared his bulk against the wood and shouldered the _________.

A. flood	B. barricade	C. purchase	D. concentration	E. comrades

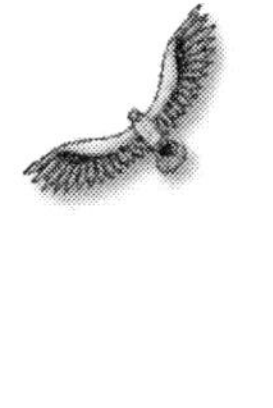

ANSWERS

WORKSHEETS 1 – 21 (Pages 1 – 70)

WORKSHEET 1

SECTION 1 CLOZE		SECTION 2 SYNONYMS	SECTION 3 SHUFFLED SENTENCES
1. E	6. G	11. B	16. very – *My family gets together every Christmas.*
2. I	7. D	12. D	17. took – *I pretended not to notice how dirty the place was.*
3. A	8. H	13. A	18. a – *Chocolate should only be eaten in small quantities.*
4. J	9. F	14. C	19. mustn't – *Don't irritate your brother while he's studying.*
5. C	10. B	15. B	20. over – *You should look after your teeth from a young age.*

WORKSHEET 2

SECTION 1 COMPREHENSION		SECTION 2 WORD DEFINITIONS	SECTION 3 COMPOUND WORDS	SECTION 4 LINKED WORDS	SECTION 5 ODD WORD OUT
1. A	6. C	11. C	16. tea, pot	21. D	26. C
2. B	7. A	12. A	17. hall, way	22. A	27. B
3. B	8. C	13. B	18. suit, case	23. C	28. D
4. D	9. B	14. D	19. back, yard	24. B	29. A
5. A	10. A	15. C	20. up, stairs	25. D	30. C

WORKSHEET 3

SECTION 1 JUMBLED PARAGRAPHS	SECTION 2 CLOZE	SECTION 3 MISSING LETTERS	SECTION 4 ADJECTIVES
1. D	6. C	11. B	16. A
2. B	7. B	12. D	17. B
3. A	8. A	13. A	18. B
4. C	9. B	14. D	19. C
5. B	10. D	15. C	20. C

WORKSHEET 4

SECTION 1 COMPREHENSION		SECTION 2 WORD DEFINITIONS	SECTION 3 ANAGRAMS	SECTION 4 LINKED WORDS	SECTION 5 SPELLING ERRORS
1. C	6. B	11. B	16. perfect	21. C	26. C – conceited
2. A	7. D	12. D	17. gum	22. B	27. A – proficiency
3. D	8. C	13. B	18. bin	23. A	28. E – courteously
4. B	9. A	14. A	19. could	24. C	29. C – exceptional
5. D	10. D	15. C	20. rules	25. D	30. A – raucous

WORKSHEET 5

SECTION 1 HOMOPHONES	SECTION 2 PARTIAL ANTONYMS	SECTION 3 SPELLING ERRORS	SECTION 4 ODD WORD OUT
1. B	6. attentive	11. B – steadfastly	16. D
2. D	7. confine	12. A – uncanny	17. A
3. C	8. friendship	13. C – reactively	18. E
4. A	9. gradual	14. C – beckoning	19. C
5. D	10. unbelievable	15. A – grub	20. B

WORKSHEET 6

SECTION 1 COMPREHENSION		SECTION 2 COMPOUND WORDS	SECTION 3 WORD DEFINITIONS	SECTION 4 ADJECTIVES	SECTION 5 RHYMING
1. A	6. C	11. B	16. B	21. C	26. straggling
2. C	7. D	12. C	17. E	22. B	27. coaxed
3. A	8. C	13. A	18. D	23. D	28. grudge
4. B	9. A	14. D	19. A	24. A	29. delirious
5. C	10. D	15. B	20. C	25. D	30. gasped

WORKSHEET 7

SECTION 1 ANAGRAMS	SECTION 2 CHANGE ONE LETTER	SECTION 3 CLOZE	SECTION 4 ANTONYMS
1. ascent	6. slurred	11. prodigious	16. B
2. traces	7. mutter	12. underestimated	17. D
3. marine	8. waiting	13. deceive	18. D
4. staple	9. recline	14. reclaim	19. D
5. lemons	10. bequest	15. prevailed	20. D

WORKSHEET 8

SECTION 1 COMPREHENSION	SECTION 2 WORD DEFINITIONS	SECTION 3 SHUFFLED SENTENCES	SECTION 4 SYNONYM GROUPS	SECTION 5 HOMOPHONES
1. B 2. C 3. A 4. C 5. C 6. C 7. C 8. C 9. A 10. C	11. A 12. C 13. D 14. A 15. D	16. and – *The suspects loitered around the building.* 17. when – *The football player received criticism for feigning an injury.* 18. would – *He often imitated his brother.* 19. when – *I'm not interested in learning all the names of different plants even though I like gardening.* 20. although – *I watched the birds playing in puddles of water.*	21. A 22. C 23. D 24. C 25. A	26. serial 27. heir 28. colonel 29. meddle 30. complement

WORKSHEET 9

SECTION 1 MISSING LETTERS	SECTION 2 CLOZE	SECTION 3 VOCABULARY IN CONTEXT	SECTION 4 PARTIAL ANTONYMS
1. B 2. C 3. D 4. B 5. C	6. diluted 7. inferior 8. competent 9. smite 10. combined	11. A 12. C 13. B 14. A 15. D	16. harmony 17. peace 18. understandable 19. eloquent 20. agreement

WORKSHEET 10

SECTION 1 COMPREHENSION		SECTION 2 LINKED WORDS	SECTION 3 COMPOUND WORDS	SECTION 4 ODD WORD OUT	SECTION 5 ANAGRAMS
1. B 2. A 3. D 4. A 5. C	6. A 7. B 8. D 9. B 10. A	11. B 12. E 13. D 14. A 15. D	16. eye, glasses 17. finger, tips 18. choke, hold 19. up, right 20. break, through	21. C 22. D 23. A 24. D 25. A	26. stable 27. thread 28. Stifle 29. caters 30. drapes

WORKSHEET 11

SECTION 1 ADJECTIVES	SECTION 2 SPELLING ERRORS	SECTION 3 WORD DEFINITIONS	SECTION 4 PARTIAL SYNONYMS
1. B 2. D 3. A 4. B 5. C	6. B – instantaneous 7. C – surreptitious 8. E – emphatic 9. D – worrisome 10. A – haphazardly	11. D 12. B 13. A 14. C 15. D	16. shriek 17. heartbroken 18. mimic 19. arbitrarily 20. brutal

WORKSHEET 12

SECTION 1 COMPREHENSION		SECTION 2 CHANGE ONE LETTER	SECTION 3 PARTIAL WORDS	SECTION 4 CLOZE	SECTION 5 SPELLING ERRORS
1. D 2. A 3. B 4. B 5. D	6. B 7. D 8. A 9. B 10. C	11. outraged 12. jilted 13. livid 14. slant 15. fleeting	16. concoct 17. understated 18. gorgeous 19. intolerable 20. profuse	21. D 22. C 23. A 24. E 25. B	26. D – immoral 27. E – capacious 28. B – ferocious 29. A – mesmerise 30. C – fortuitous

WORKSHEET 13

SECTION 1 LINKED WORDS	SECTION 2 CLOZE	SECTION 3 SHUFFLED SENTENCES	SECTION 4 SYNONYMS
1. D 2. B 3. A 4. E 5. E	6. B 7. C 8. E 9. A 10. D	11. middle – *The renegade rode his motorbike through the countryside.* 12. melting – *The temperature plummeted before we even knew.* 13. are – *Your ineptitude is really starting to annoy me.* 14. away – *Stop your larking and wash those dishes now.* 15. ponder – *I was wondering what to have for dinner.*	16. B 17. A 18. C 19. D 20. B

WORKSHEET 14

SECTION 1 COMPREHENSION		SECTION 2 CLOZE	SECTION 3 WORD DEFINITIONS	SECTION 4 PARTIAL ANTONYMS	SECTION 5 RHYMING
1. C	6. B	11. B	16. F	21. extravagant	26. declined
2. B	7. C	12. D	17. A	22. measly	27. pleasure
3. D	8. B	13. A	18. I	23. erratic	28. shrewd
4. C	9. C	14. C	19. D	24. column	29. perplexed
5. A	10. D	15. A	20. G	25. ostentatious	30. wandered

WORKSHEET 15

SECTION 1 MISSING LETTERS	SECTION 2 JUMBLED PARAGRAPHS	SECTION 3 VOCABULARY IN CONTEXT	SECTION 4 ODD WORD OUT
1. A	6. A	11. C	16. C
2. C	7. C	12. A	17. B
3. D	8. C	13. B	18. D
4. A	9. D	14. E	19. B
5. C	10. A	15. C	20. D

WORKSHEET 16

SECTION 1 COMPREHENSION	SECTION 2 SPELLING ERRORS	SECTION 3 WORD DEFINITIONS	SECTION 4 SHUFFLED SENTENCES	SECTION 5 PARTIAL SYNONYMS
1. A	11. E – hospitality	16. pensive	21. watches – *He likes to collect vinyl records in his free time.*	26. C
2. D	12. C – trek	17. scolded	22. patient – *The desert climate is unforgiving to all but the toughest.*	27. A
3. C	13. B – lugubrious	18. ample	23. rig – *The company focuses primarily on the extraction of crude oil.*	28. D
4. C	14. A – inseparable	19. mortified	24. compose – *They had to traverse the barren wastelands in a wagon.*	29. C
5. B	15. D – clamour	20. ensuing	25. a – *I feel absolutely no obligation to negotiate with unsavoury characters.*	30. C
6. C				
7. A				
8. C				
9. C				
10. D				

WORKSHEET 17

SECTION 1 ADJECTIVES	SECTION 2 HOMOPHONES	SECTION 3 LINKED WORDS	SECTION 4 CLOZE
1. B	6. D	11. C	16. contrition
2. B	7. B	12. E	17. puny
3. A	8. C	13. A	18. threshold
4. B	9. C	14. D	19. cavernous
5. D	10. D	15. E	20. subordinate

WORKSHEET 18

SECTION 1 COMPREHENSION		SECTION 2 SPELLING ERRORS	SECTION 3 ANAGRAMS	SECTION 4 PARTIAL ANTONYMS	SECTION 5 WORD SWAP
1. C	6. C	11. A – grievous	16. leading	21. explicitly	26. D, G
2. B	7. B	12. A – semblance	17. tirades	22. reveal	27. B, H
3. A	8. A	13. B – ceremoniously	18. traders	23. transient	28. D, E
4. B	9. C	14. C – inconspicuous	19. parties	24. decent	29. D, G
5. B	10. D	15. E – transitory	20. largely	25. apathy	30. B, G

WORKSHEET 19

SECTION 1 ANTONYM PAIRS	SECTION 2 SYNONYMS	SECTION 3 CLOZE	SECTION 4 WORD DEFINITIONS
1. A	6. D	11. C	16. B
2. C	7. B	12. D	17. C
3. E	8. A	13. B	18. D
4. A	9. D	14. A	19. B
5. E	10. B	15. A	20. A

WORKSHEET 20	SECTION 1 COMPREHENSION		SECTION 2 LINKED WORDS	SECTION 3 VOCABULARY IN CONTEXT	SECTION 4 SPELLING ERRORS	SECTION 5 COMPOUND WORDS
	1. D	6. B	11. B	16. C	21. B – opportunity	26. bathroom
	2. B	7. D	12. D	17. A	22. B – apprehension	27. anything
	3. A	8. B	13. B	18. D	23. C – capricious	28. somehow
	4. B	9. C	14. A	19. B	24. D – pliant	29. weekend
	5. D	10. A	15. C	20. A	25. E – reimburse	30. earpiece

WORKSHEET 21	SECTION 1 COMPOUND WORDS	SECTION 2 WORD DEFINITIONS	SECTION 3 WORD DEFINITIONS	SECTION 4 ANTONYM PAIRS
	1. D	6. D	11. G	16. A
	2. B	7. A	12. C	17. C
	3. A	8. B	13. B	18. E
	4. C	9. B	14. I	19. C
	5. D	10. A	15. F	20. E

REVISION TESTS 1 – 21 (Pages 73 – 134)

REVISION TEST 1	SECTION 1 COMPREHENSION		SECTION 2 SYNONYMS	SECTION 3 COMPOUND WORDS	SECTION 4 LINKED WORDS	SECTION 5 ODD WORD OUT
	1. A	6. A	11. C	16. handsome	21. E	26. B
	2. B	7. B	12. A	17. businessman	22. B	27. C
	3. A	8. D	13. D	18. goosebumps	23. A	28. D
	4. C	9. B	14. E	19. armchair	24. D	29. A
	5. B	10. C	15. C	20. apprenticeship	25. A	30. B

REVISION TEST 2	SECTION 1 JUMBLED PARAGRAPHS	SECTION 2 CLOZE	SECTION 3 MISSING LETTERS	SECTION 4 ADJECTIVES
	1. B	6. intent	11. D	16. D
	2. C	7. towards	12. C	17. B
	3. A	8. obedient	13. B	18. D
	4. B	9. makeshift	14. D	19. C
	5. B	10. almighty	15. A	20. E

REVISION TEST 3	SECTION 1 COMPREHENSION		SECTION 2 WORD DEFINITIONS	SECTION 3 ANAGRAMS	SECTION 4 LINKED WORDS	SECTION 5 SPELLING ERRORS
	1. B	6. A	11. D	16. nice	21. C	26. A – literally
	2. A	7. C	12. B	17. pursed	22. B	27. D – disarray
	3. C	8. D	13. A	18. grin	23. E	28. E – government
	4. C	9. C	14. E	19. debris	24. B	29. B – miscellaneous
	5. B	10. B	15. C	20. barely	25. A	30. C – almighty

REVISION TEST 4	SECTION 1 HOMOPHONES	SECTION 2 ANTONYMS	SECTION 3 SPELLING ERRORS	SECTION 4 ODD WORD OUT
	1. D	6. B	11. A – shrivelled	16. C
	2. C	7. D	12. C – incessant	17. A
	3. B	8. B	13. D – absolute	18. D
	4. A	9. A	14. A – indecisive	19. B
	5. C	10. C	15. E – magnificent	20. C

REVISION TEST 5

SECTION 1 COMPREHENSION		SECTION 2 COMPOUND WORDS	SECTION 3 REPLACE THE WORD	SECTION 4 ADJECTIVES	SECTION 5 RHYMING
1. B	6. B	11. somehow	16. C – mistake	21. C	26. national
2. C	7. A	12. heartbroken	17. B – shrewd	22. D	27. brittle
3. C	8. C	13. fingerprint	18. D – found	23. E	28. insistent
4. B	9. C	14. girlfriend	19. A – ruthlessness	24. B	29. blanked
5. B	10. D	15. understated	20. E – shifting	25. D	30. generic

REVISION TEST 6

SECTION 1 ANAGRAMS	SECTION 2 CHANGE ONE LETTER	SECTION 3 CLOZE	SECTION 4 ANTONYMS
1. subtle	6. cope	11. D	16. B
2. dent	7. dent	12. C	17. D
3. flit	8. shave	13. E	18. A
4. flair	9. wail	14. A	19. C
5. loyal	10. goad	15. E	20. B

REVISION TEST 7

SECTION 1 COMPREHENSION	SECTION 2 REPLACE THE WORD	SECTION 3 SHUFFLED SENTENCES	SECTION 4 SYNONYMS	SECTION 5 HOMOPHONES
1. A	11. B – dimly	16. the – *Anger burned his throat in a bitter stream of bile.*	21. B	26. peek
2. D	12. D – plunged	17. eating – *Claire enjoyed the unfamiliar and sedate rural views.*	22. C	27. sign
3. C	13. E – skidded	18. greasy – *Emerging on the other side, she saw undulating hills.*	23. B	28. lie
4. B	14. A – delved	19. likewise – *It felt like the first week of the summer holidays.*	24. D	29. passed
5. A	15. C – eluding	20. for – *Claire peered through the window, looking for Gladys.*	25. B	30. feint
6. B				
7. D				
8. C				
9. A				
10. C				

REVISION TEST 8

SECTION 1 MISSING LETTERS	SECTION 2 SPELLING ERRORS	SECTION 3 CLOZE	
1. C	6. D – colossal	11. E	16. D
2. D	7. A – chiselled	12. J	17. I
3. A	8. D – intricate	13. C	18. H
4. D	9. B – unforeseen	14. F	19. G
5. B	10. E – exhilarating	15. A	20. B

REVISION TEST 9

SECTION 1 COMPREHENSION		SECTION 2 LINKED WORDS	SECTION 3 COMPOUND WORDS	SECTION 4 ODD WORD OUT	SECTION 5 ANAGRAMS
1. A	6. D	11. D	16. football	21. B	26. glare
2. B	7. D	12. C	17. cupboard	22. D	27. three
3. C	8. C	13. B	18. doughnut	23. B	28. spoiled
4. B	9. A	14. B	19. earshot	24. A	29 courteous
5. C	10. B	15. B	20. hairdresser	25. C	30. kitchen

REVISION TEST 10

SECTION 1 ADJECTIVES	SECTION 2 SPELLING ERRORS	SECTION 3 RHYMING	SECTION 4 REPLACE THE WORD
1. D	6. D – ludicrous	11. swirled	16. B – warranted
2. B	7. D – succeed	12. protectively	17. D – scrawled
3. B	8. E – capability	13. investigated	18. C – perched
4. D	9. C – occasion	14. flouncing	19. E – blithely
5. C	10. B – instigate	15. spaghetti	20. A – suspiciously

REVISION TEST 11

SECTION 1 COMPREHENSION		SECTION 2 CHANGE ONE LETTER	SECTION 3 PARTIAL WORDS	SECTION 4 CLOZE	SECTION 5 PARTIAL ANTONYMS
1. B	6. C	11. blushing	16. octogenarian	21. B	26. D
2. C	7. A	12. alien	17. ruffle	22. E	27. B
3. C	8. C	13. cram	18. croak	23. D	28. E
4. D	9. A	14. muse	19. mischief	24. A	29. C
5. A	10. C	15. slick	20. deck	25. C	30. A

REVISION TEST 12

SECTION 1 LINKED WORDS	SECTION 2 CLOZE	SECTION 3 WORD SWAP	SECTION 4 SYNONYMS
1. B	6. B	11. E, H	16. C
2. E	7. A	12. A, G	17. D
3. D	8. C	13. C, H	18. B
4. C	9. E	14. C, G	19. A
5. A	10. D	15. D, G	20. C

REVISION TEST 13

SECTION 1 COMPREHENSION		SECTION 2 RHYMING	SECTION 3 WORD SWAP	SECTION 4 SYNONYM GROUPS	SECTION 5 ADJECTIVES
1. D	6. A	11. hesitation	16. D, H	21. A	26. D
2. B	7. B	12. bracelet	17. D, G	22. D	27. C
3. C	8. D	13. pride	18. C, F	23. C	28. D
4. B	9. B	14. obligation	19. B, E	24. A	29. B
5. A	10. C	15. decommissioned	20. A, H	25. A	30. A

REVISION TEST 14

SECTION 1 MISSING LETTERS	SECTION 2 JUMBLED PARAGRAPHS	SECTION 3 VOCABULARY IN CONTEXT	SECTION 4 ODD WORD OUT
1. B	6. C	11. C	16. B
2. D	7. B	12. B	17. D
3. C	8. D	13. E	18. A
4. A	9. A	14. B	19. B
5. D	10. C	15. A	20. D

REVISION TEST 15

SECTION 1 COMPREHENSION	SECTION 2 SPELLING ERRORS	SECTION 3 WORD DEFINITIONS	SECTION 4 SYNONYM	SECTION 5 SHUFFLED SENTENCES
1. A	11. D – advanced	16. C	21. B	26. skip – *Jack scaled the steep steps two at a time.*
2. D	12. D – commuter	17. C	22. A	27. down – *Her gullible sister had fallen for Josh Drane.*
3. B	13. A – irresistible	18. B	23. D	28. you – *My kung fu master says you reap what you sow in this world.*
4. D	14. E – heightened	19. A	24. C	29. super – *She never took the invitation for granted.*
5. B	15. E – sombre	20. E	25. B	30. the – *Claire left her bag in the hall.*
6. B				
7. C				
8. A				
9. C				
10. B				

REVISION TEST 16

SECTION 1 ADJECTIVES	SECTION 2 HOMOPHONES	SECTION 3 LINKED WORDS	SECTION 4 CLOZE
1. D	6. wail	11. C	16. earnest
2. B	7. waive	12. C	17. willed
3. E	8. knight	13. A	18. deserted
4. A	9. meat	14. C	19. supposed
5. D	10. taut	15. A	20. futile

REVISION TEST 17

SECTION 1 COMPREHENSION		SECTION 2 SPELLING ERRORS	SECTION 3 ANAGRAMS	SECTION 4 ANTONYMS	SECTION 5 CHANGE ONE LETTER
1. B	6. A	11. A – compel	16. fingers	21. C	26. stoop
2. D	7. A	12. D – consistent	17. scrub	22. A	27. speck
3. D	8. A	13. C – guarded	18. forward	23. C	28. levy
4. B	9. C	14. A – absence	19. strolled	24. C	29. sense
5. C	10. B	15. D – jeopardy	20. pages	25. D	30. clamber

REVISION TEST 18

SECTION 1 ODD WORD OUT	SECTION 2 SYNONYMS	SECTION 3 CLOZE	SECTION 4 PARTIAL WORDS
1. B	6. C	11. expensive	16. heroic
2. A	7. A	12. scrounging	17. impulsive
3. D	8. D	13. wardrobe	18. volatile
4. D	9. A	14. trainers	19. selfish
5. D	10. B	15. snipe	20. sequester

REVISION TEST 19

SECTION 1 COMPREHENSION		SECTION 2 LINKED WORDS	SECTION 3 VOCABULARY IN CONTEXT	SECTION 4 COMPOUND WORDS	SECTION 5 HOMOPHONES
1. D	6. A	11. D	16. B	21. C	26. D
2. A	7. C	12. E	17. D	22. D	27. C
3. B	8. D	13. C	18. A	23. A	28. B
4. A	9. A	14. E	19. D	24. C	29. A
5. D	10. B	15. C	20. E	25. D	30. D

REVISION TEST 20

SECTION 1 COMPOUND WORDS	SECTION 2 WORD SWAP	SECTION 3 REPLACE THE WORD	SECTION 4 ANTONYMS
1. B	6. foliage, grasped	11. E – turned	16. C
2. D	7. halt, she	12. B – alone	17. D
3. B	8. ankles, grab	13. A – tip	18. C
4. C	9. unrelenting, stopped	14. C – uninspiring	19. D
5. C	10. his, her	15. D – jabbed	20. C

REVISION TEST 21

SECTION 1 COMPREHENSION	SECTION 2 PARTIAL SYNONYMS	SECTION 3 SHUFFLED SENTENCES	SECTION 4 VOCABULARY IN CONTEXT	SECTION 5 CLOZE
1. D	11. perpetually	16. with – *Claire stiffened, staring at the carpet.*	21. C	26. D
2. B	12. rarely	17. the – *She gingerly lifted him to avoid more damage.*	22. A	27. B
3. C	13. regard	18. in – *Her face wore a mixture of love and sorrow.*	23. B	28. C
4. B	14. repugnance	19. and – *I'm going to wet this flannel with freezing water.*	24. D	29. E
5. A	15. inspire	20. into – *She ducked through the bathroom door and locked it.*	25. D	30. B
6. C				
7. D				
8. A				
9. D				
10. D				

Learn With *The Cadwaladr Quests* Series

Your ***11+ Vocabulary, Comprehension and Verbal Skills - Workbook 1*** forms part of
The Cadwaladr Quests
integrated education series.

While this book functions as a fully standalone workbook, you may want to read Book 1 in the series – the original vocabulary novel ***Tangled Time*** – then consolidate your comprehension, vocabulary and verbal skills with this workbook for a more effective approach. Finally, further test your knowledge with the *Vocabulary Revision Notebook.*

Improve even further, with the subsequent volumes in the series!

Find all the available *The Cadwaladr Quests Series* books online via your local Amazon store.

The Cadwaladr Quests – Book 1 – Tangled Time

Further learning books:
The Cadwaladr Quests – Book 1 – Tangled Time – Workbook
The Cadwaladr Quests – Book 1 – Tangled Time – Vocabulary Revision Notebook

The Cadwaladr Quests – Book 2 – Race For The Gold

Further learning books:
The Cadwaladr Quests – Book 2 – Race For The Gold – Workbook
The Cadwaladr Quests – Book 2 – Race For The Gold – Vocabulary Revision Notebook

Reviews, Please!

If you've enjoyed *the* ***11+ Vocabulary, Comprehension and Verbal Skills – Workbook 1***, please feel free to leave a review online at the book's Amazon page.

Errata and Information

To report any errata[1], please email: errata@slager.co.uk
If you would like information about new books in ***The Cadwaladr Quests*** series, please visit:

SLAGER.CO.UK

You can stay up to date with S.L. Ager, author of ***The Cadwaladr Quests*** series, on social media:

facebook.com/SLAgerAuthor
instagram.com/SLAgerAuthor
linkedin.com/in/SlagerAuthor
pinterest.com/SLAgerAuthor
twitter.com/SLAgerAuthor

For further information about **XLEducation**, please visit:

XL-EDUCATION.CO.UK

[1] erratum *(n)* an error in writing or publishing (plural: *errata*).

Manufactured by Amazon.ca
Bolton, ON